AMPHIBIANS
of the PACIFIC NORTHWEST

Lawrence L.C. Jones, William P. Leonard
and Deanna H. Olson, editors

Seattle Audubon Society
for birds and nature

Front Cover: Northern Red-legged Frog (photograph by Klaus O. Richter)
Back Cover (left to right): Wood Frog (photograph by Larry West), Boreal Chorus Frog egg mass (photograph by Kirwin Werner), California Newt (photograph by Wayne Van Devender)

ISBN 0-914516-16-7 $19.95

Published by Seattle Audubon Society
Production editing by Constance Sidles
Design by Lorie Ransom
Production layouts by Nick Gregoric
Maps by Richard S. Nauman and Lorie Ransom
Line drawings by Lorie Ransom

Printed in Hong Kong by Mantec Production Company

Sponsored by:
Society for Northwestern Vertebrate Biology
USDA Forest Service

To obtain additional copies of this book, write or call:

Seattle Audubon Society   (206)523-4483
8050 35th Avenue NE
Seattle, WA 98115

www.seattleaudubon.org

*While a great many biologists have contributed
to our knowledge of the herpetofauna of the Pacific Northwest, the
editors would like to recognize the long-term contributions of four
people—three of whom we are honored to have as authors in this field
guide. R. Bruce Bury, Robert C. Stebbins, Robert M. Storm and
David B. Wake have been herpetological mainstays in the
Pacific Northwest. They have enriched our understanding of
amphibians and reptiles and have been pivotal inspirations to
researchers, students, natural history buffs and the public.
Their professional dedication and enthusiasm have been unwavering
and contagious. We dedicate this book to them.*

*—Lawrence L.C. Jones, William P. Leonard
and Deanna H. Olson, editors*

TABLE OF CONTENTS

▢ FROGS AND TOADS, ANURA

TAILED FROGS, Ascaphidae

SPADEFOOT TOADS, Pelobatidae

TRUE TOADS, Bufonidae

TREEFROGS, Hylidae

TRUE FROGS, Ranidae

218 References

SPECIES CHECKLIST

CLASS **Amphibians** (AMPHIBIA)

ORDER **Salamanders** (CAUDATA)

FAMILY **Mole Salamanders** (AMBYSTOMATIDAE)
- [ ] Northwestern Salamander (*Ambystoma gracile*)
- [ ] Long-toed Salamander (*Ambystoma macrodactylum*)
- [ ] Tiger Salamander (*Ambystoma tigrinum*)

FAMILY **Pacific Giant Salamanders** (DICAMPTODONTIDAE)
- [ ] Idaho Giant Salamander (*Dicamptodon aterrimus*)
- [ ] Cope's Giant Salamander (*Dicamptodon copei*)
- [ ] California Giant Salamander (*Dicamptodon ensatus*)
- [ ] Coastal Giant Salamander (*Dicamptodon tenebrosus*)

FAMILY **Torrent Salamanders** (RHYACOTRITONIDAE)
- [ ] Cascade Torrent Salamander (*Rhyacotriton cascadae*)
- [ ] Columbia Torrent Salamander (*Rhyacotriton kezeri*)
- [ ] Olympic Torrent Salamander (*Rhyacotriton olympicus*)
- [ ] Southern Torrent Salamander (*Rhyacotriton variegatus*)

FAMILY **Newts** (SALAMANDRIDAE)
- [ ] Rough-skinned Newt (*Taricha granulosa*)
- [ ] Red-bellied Newt (*Taricha rivularis*)
- [ ] California Newt (*Taricha torosa*)

FAMILY **Lungless Salamanders** (PLETHODONTIDAE)

GENUS **Climbing Salamanders** (*Aneides*)
- [ ] Clouded Salamander (*Aneides ferreus*)
- [ ] Black Salamander (*Aneides flavipunctatus*)
- [ ] Arboreal Salamander (*Aneides lugubris*)
- [ ] Wandering Salamander (*Aneides vagrans*)

GENUS **Slender Salamanders** (*Batrachoseps*)
- [ ] California Slender Salamander (*Batrachoseps attenuatus*)
- [ ] Oregon Slender Salamander (*Batrachoseps wrighti*)

GENUS **Ensatinas** (*Ensatina*)
- [ ] Ensatina (*Ensatina eschscholtzii*)

GENUS **Web-toed Salamanders** (*Hydromantes*)
- [ ] Shasta Salamander (*Hydromantes shastae*)

GENUS **Woodland Salamanders** (*Plethodon*)
- [ ] Scott Bar Salamander (*Plethodon asupak*)
- [ ] Dunn's Salamander (*Plethodon dunni*)
- [ ] Del Norte Salamander (*Plethodon elongatus*)
- [ ] Coeur d'Alene Salamander (*Plethodon idahoensis*)

SPECIES CHECKLIST

☐ Larch Mountain Salamander *(Plethodon larselli)*
☐ Siskiyou Mountains Salamander *(Plethodon stormi)*
☐ Van Dyke's Salamander *(Plethodon vandykei)*
☐ Western Red-backed Salamander *(Plethodon vehiculum)*

ORDER	**Frogs and Toads** (ANURA)
FAMILY	**Tailed Frogs** (ASCAPHIDAE)

☐ Rocky Mountain Tailed Frog *(Ascaphus montanus)*
☐ Coastal Tailed Frog *(Ascaphus truei)*

FAMILY	**Spadefoot Toads** (PELOBATIDAE)

☐ Great Basin Spadefoot *(Spea intermontana)*

FAMILY	**True Toads** (BUFONIDAE)

☐ Western Toad *(Bufo boreas)*
☐ Woodhouse's Toad *(Bufo woodhousii)*

FAMILY	**Treefrogs** (HYLIDAE)

☐ Boreal Chorus Frog *(Pseudacris maculata)*
☐ Pacific Treefrog *(Pseudacris regilla)*

FAMILY	**True Frogs** (RANIDAE)

☐ Northern Red-legged Frog *(Rana aurora)*
☐ Foothill Yellow-legged Frog *(Rana boylii)*
☐ Cascades Frog *(Rana cascadae)*
☐ Bullfrog *(Rana catesbeiana)* (I)
☐ Green Frog *(Rana clamitans)* (I)
☐ California Red-legged Frog *(Rana draytonii)*
☐ Columbia Spotted Frog *(Rana luteiventris)*
☐ Northern Leopard Frog *(Rana pipiens)*
☐ Oregon Spotted Frog *(Rana pretiosa)*
☐ Wood Frog *(Rana sylvatica)*

(I) *Species introduced to the Pacific Northwest*

Publisher's Preface

Amphibians of the Pacific Northwest is the most recent in the long and rich history of Seattle Audubon Society's publications in support of our mission to cultivate and lead a community that values and protects birds and the natural environment. These publications engage us in Seattle Audubon's vision of a healthy environment in balance with nature, where people enjoy, respect and care for the natural resources that sustain the community of life. *Amphibians of the Pacific Northwest* is a new book that expands on the previous *Amphibians of Washington and Oregon,* published by Seattle Audubon Society in 1993.

Seattle Audubon Publications Committee members Constance Sidles (production editor), Lorie Ransom (designer) and Nick Gregoric (production artist) deserve our special thanks for their contributions to the professional design, layout and production of this book. The Seattle Audubon Society also thanks those who generously donated the content of this book: the manuscripts, the maps and one-time use of photographs. Special thanks go to editors Lawrence L.C. Jones, William P. Leonard and Deanna H. Olson. William P. Leonard in particular worked tirelessly with the Publications Committee on every aspect of the book. We also wish to thank the USDA Forest Service and the Society for Northwestern Vertebrate Biology for their support and financial assistance.

For other books published by the Seattle Audubon Society, or for membership and other information on the work of Seattle Audubon, please see our web site at www.seattleaudubon.org.

—*Richard P. Youel*
Chair, Publications Committee
Seattle Audubon Society

Columbia Spotted Frog

WILLIAM LEONARD

Acknowledgements

This book would not have been possible without assistance from many people who helped in countless ways. Contributing authors of this book often did much more than write their own sections. Most also contributed their knowledge to other sections, reviewed others' text and species range maps, and provided moral support. We would like to thank them for their patience and for all that they have taught us.

So many others also contributed to this volume. For their inspiration and support, we would like to thank Char Corkran, James Harding, Mike McDowell, Brad Moon, Marty Raphael, Tom Skinner, Robert Stebbins and Chris Thoms. For their roles in our professional development, we thank Steve Herman, Ronald Nussbaum, Tim Quinn, Gordon Reeves and David Sever. For sharing their knowledge regarding amphibians in the Pacific Northwest, we thank Jim Atkinson, Joe Beatty, Tim Burkhardt, Richard Carstensen, Lowell Diller, Linda DuPuis, Ron Friesz, Laura Friis, Steve Goodman, Andrea Herman, Pierre Johnstone, Bryce Maxell, Christopher Pearl, Chuck Peterson, David Pilliod, Barry Sinervo, Jack Sullivan and Kirwin Werner. Chapters in this volume benefited from comments by Dan Beck, Kelly Burnett, David Pilliod, Kathryn Ronnenberg, Robert Weaver and Stephanie Wessell. Several individuals generously permitted us to reproduce their wonderful images in this book, including Ronn Altig, Edmund D. Brodie, Jr., James Harding, Brad Moon, Wayne Van Devender, Kirwin Werner and Larry West. Others helped us locate animals for photography; these people include Keith Aubry, Jim Baugh, Karen Danner, Lowell Diller, Fred Dobler, Ron Friesz, Steve Germaine, Garth Hodgson, Shelly Jay, Adam Jones, Megan Leonard, Nick Leonard, Vicki Leonard,

Singing male Boreal Chorus Frog

Peter Llewendal, Steve Manlow, Jerod Sapp, Chuck Peterson, Phil Peterson, Casey Richart, Heather Simmons, Kirwin Werner and Susan Whitford. Field assistance was provided by Loretta Ellenburg, Josh Jones, Matt McDowell, Shannon McDowell and Chris Knauf. Editorial support was graciously given by Janet Jones and Kathryn Ronnenberg.

Finally, it was a tremendous experience to work with the members of the Publications Committee of Seattle Audubon Society: Richard Youel, Constance Sidles, Lorie Ransom, Nick Gregoric, George Johnson, Hal Opperman, Idie Ulsh and Russell Steele. We thank you all!

—*The Authors*

Contributing Authors

Andrew R. Blaustein
Department of Zoology
3029 Cordley Hall
Oregon State University
Corvallis, OR 97331-2914

Herbert A. Brown
Biology Department
Western Washington University
Bellingham, WA 98225-9160

Evelyn L. Bull
USDA Forest Service
Pacific Northwest Research Station
1401 Gekeler Lane
La Grande, OR 97850

Gwendolynn W. Bury
USGS Forest and Rangeland
Ecosystem Science Center
3200 SW Jefferson Way
Corvallis, OR 97331

R. Bruce Bury
USGS Forest and Rangeland
Ecosystem Science Center
3200 SW Jefferson Way
Corvallis, OR 97331

David Clayton
USDA Forest Service
Rogue River-Siskiyou National Forest
333 West Eighth Street, Box 520
Medford, OR 97501

Charles M. Crisafulli
USDA Forest Service
Pacific Northwest Research Station
3625 93rd Avenue SW
Olympia, WA 98512

David M. Darda
Department of Biological Sciences
Central Washington University
400 East University Way
Ellensburg, WA 98926-7537

Theodore M. Davis
Department of Biology
Camosun College
3100 Foul Bay Road
Victoria, BC V8P 5J2 Canada

Gary M. Fellers
USGS Western Ecological
Research Center
Point Reyes National Seashore
Point Reyes, CA 94956

Lisa A. Hallock
Natural Heritage Program
Department of Natural Resources
1111 Washington Street SE
P.O. Box 47014
Olympia, WA 98504-7014

Marc P. Hayes
Science Division, Habitat Program
Washington Department of
Fish and Wildlife
600 Capitol Way North
Olympia, WA 98501-1091

Lynne Houck
Department of Zoology
3029 Cordley Hall
Oregon State University
Corvallis, OR 97331-2914

Mark R. Jennings
Rana Resources
39913 Sharon Avenue
Davis, CA 95616-9456

Lawrence L. C. Jones
USDA Forest Service
Pacific Northwest Research Station
3625 93rd Avenue SW
Olympia, WA 98512
current address:
USDA Forest Service
Wildlife Program
Coronado National Forest
Supervisor's Office
300 West Congress
Tucson, AZ 85735

Shawn R. Kuchta
University of California, Santa Cruz
Ecology & Evolutionary Biology
Earth & Marine Sciences, Room A316
Santa Cruz, CA 95064

Sarah J. Kupferberg
Questa Engineering
P.O. Box 70356
1220 Brickyard Cove Road, Suite 206
Pt. Richmond, CA 94807

William P. Leonard
Washington State Department
of Transportation
Environmental Services Office
P.O. Box 47331
Olympia, WA 98504-7331

Amy J. Lind
USDA Forest Service
Pacific Southwest Research Station
Sierra Nevada Research Center
2121 Second Street, Suite A-101
Davis, CA 95616

Kelly R. McAllister
Washington Department of
Fish and Wildlife
600 Capitol Way North
Olympia, WA 98501-1091

Louise S. Mead
Section of Ecology and Evolution
2320 Storer Hall
University of California, Davis
Davis, CA 95616

Richard S. Nauman
USDA Forest Service
Pacific Northwest Research Station
3200 SW Jefferson Way
Corvallis, OR 97331

Deanna H. Olson
USDA Forest Service
Pacific Northwest Research Station
3200 SW Jefferson Way
Corvallis, OR 97331

Kristiina Ovaska
Biolinx Environmental Research Limited
4180 Clinton Place
Victoria, BC V8Z 6M1 Canada

Klaus O. Richter
King County Department of
Natural Resources
201 South Jackson Street, Suite 600
Seattle, WA 98194

Kevin R. Russell
College of Natural Resources
University of Wisconsin
Stevens Point, WI 54481

Matthew Snook
Oregon Department of Fish and Wildlife
211 Inlow Hall
Eastern Oregon University
1 University Blvd.
La Grande, OR 98750

Robert M. Storm
1623 SW Brooklane Drive
Corvallis, OR 97313

R. Steven Wagner
Department of Biological Sciences
Central Washington University
400 East University Way
Ellensburg, WA 98926-7537

David B. Wake
Department of Integrative Biology,
and Museum of Vertebrate Zoology
3101 Valley Life Sciences Building
University of California
Berkeley, CA 94720-3160

Hartwell H. Welsh, Jr.
USDA Forest Service
Pacific Southwest Research Station
Redwood Sciences Laboratory
1700 Bayview Drive
Arcata, CA 95521

Albert G. Wilson, Jr.
Department of Biology
Spokane Falls Community College
3410 Fort George Wright Drive
Spokane, WA 99224

Elke Wind
E. Wind Consulting
348 Machleary Street
Nanaimo, BC Canada V9R 2G9

Northern Red-legged Frog

INTRODUCTION

Biology is an evolving science, constantly changing as new information is accumulated and interpreted. Throughout the late twentieth and early twenty-first centuries, our understanding of the taxonomy, ecology and conservation needs of Pacific Northwest amphibians has burgeoned.

To stay current, field guides must be "living documents" that are revised periodically to incorporate new information. In this book, we have not only provided updated species information, we have expanded the scope of the traditional regional field guide. Two novel aspects of this book are its synthesis of knowledge and its geographic scope. We have compiled a body of knowledge that has never before been attempted, using the scientific expertise of 33 contributing authors, in addition to other experts who were consulted. Our intent is to provide a new synthesis of the regional fauna, well grounded in science but presented in an integrated, readable package.

The geographic scope of this book uses ecologically relevant boundaries encompassing a distinct herpetofaunal assemblage, rather than traditional political borders. The Pacific Northwest is defined here as the lands along the Pacific Coast from Alaska and the Yukon in the north to the coastal mountains in the vicinity of Santa Cruz, California (excluding the Central Valley and Sierra Nevada) in the south, and eastward to the Siskiyou Mountains and northern Rocky Mountains of southeastern British Columbia, Idaho and western Montana.

The arid and mountainous areas to the south and east, as well as the relatively harsh interior continental climate, have served to isolate Northwest amphibians. Within the Northwest, geology and climate have further restricted the geographic ranges of individual species of amphibians.

This book includes a species account and color photos of each of the 47 native and naturalized species known to occur in the Northwest. Three species that may be encountered at the southern limits of our area but are not included in this book are the Gabilan Mountains Slender Salamander (*Batrachoseps gavilanensis*), Western Spadefoot (*Spea hammondii*) and California Tiger Salamander (*Ambystoma californiense*), as these are indicative of the more xeric climates of the California Central Valley and/or the southern California Coast Ranges. However, because a few populations of the California Tiger Salamander do spill over into our area, we have included information on it in the Remarks section of the Tiger Salamander species account, a species with which it is closely allied. For more information on these and other peripheral species, refer to some of the books in our General References section.

Using This Book

We offer this guide to assist students, teachers, naturalists and field biologists with a basic understanding and field identification of the amphibians of the Pacific Northwest. This book contains several introductory chapters intended to provide background information on Northwest amphibians. We recommend that you read these chapters before diving into the species accounts, in order to gain a better understanding of amphibian biology and habitat use.

Immediately following these chapters are the individual species accounts. Within the salamander and frog/toad sections, the species accounts are arranged taxonomically by family, then alphabetically by scientific names. The species accounts provide the necessary information to identify all of the amphibian species that are currently known to occur in the Pacific Northwest.

To identify a frog or salamander in the field, begin with a careful examination of the animal. Next, page through the species accounts in the salamander or frog/toad section, looking for the photographs that most closely resemble the species that you have observed. Once you have narrowed down the possibilities, read the Description, Variation, Similar Species and Distribution sections (including the range maps) in the species account as you attempt to further narrow the potential species through a process of elimination. These sections will provide you with the best clues as to which species you have observed.

As you read, ask yourself the following questions: (1) Does the animal match the description (including possible variations)? (2) Does the species occur within the geographical area described and mapped? (3) Can each of the similar species be ruled out? If the answer is "yes" to all these questions, you can be reasonably certain that a correct identification has been made. If in doubt, take a photograph of the specimen and seek the advice of an expert. A good quality photograph, showing key identification features, can be invaluable for this purpose.

It is important to keep in mind that in some instances, the identification of a specimen may be possible only to the genus. This problem is especially common with larval amphibians, some of which are notoriously challenging, even for experts. With increased experience and careful observation, however, you can become skilled at identifying our region's amphibians, especially adult specimens.

In the beginning, field guides will be invaluable to you, but as your knowledge and experience grow, you will find that your tattered field guides will stay on the bookshelf as references, freeing up more space for a field journal, binoculars, camera, nets and collection/observation containers.

Nomenclature

Herpetologists, those who study reptiles and amphibians ("herps" for short), have developed various species naming conventions. The common and scientific names used in this book follow those recommended by professional herpetological societies (Crother and others, 2001 and 2003 [see References]), with two exceptions. We have recognized the Northern Red-legged Frog and the California Red-legged Frog as full species (not subspecies), following Shaffer et al. (2004). We have also added the Scott Bar Salamander, following Mead and others, 2005. Finally, as per the direction in Crother and others (2001), we used initial uppercase letters for the common names of species and subspecies but not for other taxonomic levels. For example, Coastal Tailed Frog is capitalized, but references to all species of tailed frogs are not.

The reader may note that throughout the text of this book, a common name for a family is often used and typically ends with "id." For example, ranid refers to the family Ranidae (true frogs), plethodontid refers to the family Plethodontidae (lungless salamanders), and belostomatid refers to the family Belostomatidae (giant water bugs). If you are unclear as to the meaning of these common names, a web-search will usually reveal the origin.

Maps

The range maps were created using the most current information available. We did not attempt to compile museum records but instead relied on published locality maps when available, and more general range maps otherwise. The greatest efforts to review and refine the maps were made in areas within the scope of this book (see map, above right).

The distribution of some species, such as the Del Norte Salamander and the Oregon Spotted Frog, has been studied in detail, while the distribution of other species, such as the Long-toed Salamander, is less well known. The precision and accuracy of the maps are directly related to the level of knowledge of the distribution of each species. The small finished size of the maps required that the ranges be depicted in a generalized way; fine detail was not possible. Species may not be found in all areas within the range as depicted, particularly those with specialized habitat requirements. Our maps benefited greatly from recent publications and Internet resources. However, in areas of uncertainty, the author(s) of the species account made the final decisions regarding the maps of species ranges. Finally, recent field surveys

◻ Species Extent

Range of this book

and research have documented significant reductions in the range of three species: Foothill Yellow-legged Frog, Northern Leopard Frog and Oregon Spotted Frog. For these species, the maps represent both the current range, in dark shading, and the historic range, in light shading.

Photographs

We have used at least one photograph of a typical adult of each species but have also tried to show some of the variations that may be encountered in natural situations. Whenever possible, photographs of other life stages, including paedomorphs, larvae and eggs, have been shown.

LAWS AND CONSERVATION
Kelly R. McAllister and Lawrence L. C. Jones

Amphibians are a unique and integral component of Pacific Northwest ecosystems, and we have ethical and legal obligations to conserve amphibian taxa and their habitats. More than half of the species in this book have Status of Concern in some part of their range because they may be locally uncommon. Whether we merely observe species or are engaged in research, we must be cognizant of the laws and conservation measures that apply. In particular, it is important to understand the rules before handling amphibians or taking them out of their natural habitats, and these rules may change with the ownership of the land.

U.S. Protections
Virtually every U.S. state has laws that pertain to efforts to kill, capture, collect, transport, possess or commercialize wildlife. States also maintain lists of Endangered, Threatened, Sensitive, and otherwise protected species (Status of Concern). Additional policies or rules often apply to these species, providing additional levels of protection. Permits usually provide the only means to engage legally in any of the activities listed above. A permit (hunting or fishing license or scientific collecting permit) often is required to handle or collect wildlife. State permit applications are available at the state office that manages non-game wildlife species.

For protection of the rarest amphibians, the most important federal law is the Endangered Species Act (ESA), which applies to formally listed species. This law is a final stopgap measure to prevent extinction and protect those rare species with high risk to their persistence. At the present time, the California Red-legged Frog is the only federally listed amphibian in our Pacific Northwest region, although there are several candidates for listing. A federal permit is required to interact with this taxon.

The USDA Forest Service and Bureau of Land Management also have Sensitive Species programs that may require surveys prior to land management actions, as well as mitigation measures to maintain stable, well-distributed populations on federal lands, and to preclude federal listing under the ESA.

Some public and Native American lands have their own body of regulations that apply within their jurisdictions. State permits that allow collection of wildlife often are invalid within these jurisdictions. While relatively rare, some city and county parks also have restrictions prohibiting the removal of native fauna.

British Columbia Regulations
British Columbia's Wildlife Act establishes the baseline of legal protections for the province's wildlife. Capturing, killing, injuring and possessing wildlife are generally prohibited. For game animals and fish, open seasons, with bag limits and license requirements, create legal exceptions to the law. For amphibians, exceptions to the law are allowed by permit. Permits are issued by regional managers within the Wildlife Branch. Regional managers can, at their discretion, write permits which exempt an individual from the provisions of the Wildlife Act, as long as the exemption is for specific purposes such as scientific collection, education or rehabilitation.

Canada's recent Species at Risk Act is significant in that it extends protection to the "residence" or place where one or more individuals of an Endangered or Threatened Species is found. The Committee on the Status of Endangered Wildlife in Canada administers the official list of Endangered

WILLIAM LEONARD

Metamorph Columbia Spotted Frog

and Threatened Species and Species of Special Concern. At present, Endangered Species in the region include Oregon Spotted Frog, Northern Leopard Frog (southern mountain population), Rocky Mountain Tailed Frog and Tiger Salamander (southern mountain population). Threatened Species include the Coastal Giant Salamander and Great Basin Spadefoot Toad.

Environmental Ethics

As children, many of us seemed to think it was a good idea to pick up a bucketful of starfish on our trips to the beach, just to satisfy our natural curiosity about living things. We hope that our view of how we should interact with the natural world is changing as humans encroach more upon undeveloped areas. Whenever we interact with our environment, we must consider the consequences of our actions. For species about which we have conservation concerns, it may be particularly important to scrutinize our actions.

Historically, observing amphibians has often been done by wantonly flipping over cover objects (such as rocks and logs) to expose these secretive animals. This causes damage to the sensitive microenvironment that has developed below the cover object over many years. Whenever surface objects must be lifted, they must be carefully replaced, and the denizens must not be crushed. Indeed, in many situations, it is not possible to turn over an object without damaging the microenvironment.

Large, decaying logs and objects in water and talus slopes are prime examples of sensitive structures. The good news is that in most cases, cover objects need not be disturbed to observe amphibians. Many species are eminently "watchable wildlife." As birders can view wildlife through binoculars, herpers can observe their target species without harm. It is far more satisfying to observe amphibians in their natural environment than it is to see a frightened animal that just had its roof removed.

The key to good observational skills is learning when and where the animals will be, by knowing what they are doing and why. The species accounts and habitat chapters are particularly useful in this regard. Nocturnal species—for example, most salamanders—are best observed at night. Chances for observation also increase by being out at the times when the animals are surface active, such as during or after warm rains. Most "pond-breeding" amphibians are most observable when they are migrating to or from their breeding sites, or when they are engaged in courtship. Seeing a "raft" of breeding newts or a pond full of chorusing treefrogs is a memorable experience. Pacific giant salamanders are an awesome sight when you see them at night as you walk up a small stream (carefully) with a flashlight.

Many people like to keep amphibians as pets. Some species do in fact make good pets, while others do not. All species have certain moisture, temperature and food requirements, and one should never attempt to keep amphibians as pets unless one is prepared to deal with these animals in a humane, legal and responsible manner. Many Northwestern species have evolved in cool, moist conditions, and these conditions must be mimicked for successful rearing. It is best to seek guidance from taxa and husbandry experts if you wish to maintain amphibians in captivity.

BIOLOGY OF AMPHIBIANS

Overview of Amphibians
David M. Darda

Amphibians are fascinating creatures. To many people, they are relatively unknown and mysterious little animals representing some ancient evolutionary "leftover." As it turns out, amphibians are not merely remnants from the past but represent one of the most significant events in vertebrate evolution—the transition from water to land. In addition to their evolutionary significance, we are only now beginning to appreciate their diversity and importance in ecosystem function.

Diversity

A common misconception about amphibians is that there are not many kinds of them. In fact, there are approximately 5,500 species of amphibians worldwide currently recognized by herpetologists. That means that there are almost 1,000 more species of amphibians than species of mammals! Most of this diversity (approximately 4,800 species) is contained in one group of amphibians—the frogs. All frogs and toads are classified in the order Anura ("without tail"). Although they are widely distributed throughout the world, they are most abundant in the tropics. Fifteen species of frogs are native to the Pacific Northwest. Another group of amphibians, the salamanders, is classified as a second order, the Caudata ("having tail"). They are distributed throughout the north temperate regions of the world and enter the tropics only in the western hemisphere where they extend through Central America into South America. About 500 species of salamanders are currently recognized worldwide, with 30 found in the Pacific Northwest. The third group of amphibians is the least known. The caecilians of the order Gymnophiona ("naked snake") are legless amphibians that mostly burrow in the ground. This group is represented by approximately 160 species distributed only in tropical regions of the world. Except for southernmost Mexico, none occur in North America.

Hatchling Oregon Spotted Frog tadpoles

WILLIAM LEONARD

The 45 species of amphibians native to the Pacific Northwest represent only a small portion of this impressive worldwide diversity. This is not surprising because the numbers of species generally decline as one moves into the higher latitudes. Nevertheless, our region is home to some of the more interesting amphibians known. Tailed frogs, Pacific giant salamanders and torrent salamanders represent three taxa found no place else in the world. The biogeographic history of these and other Pacific Northwest amphibians is leading to a clearer understanding of evolutionary processes.

Evolution

Fossil evidence indicates that the earliest amphibians evolved from fishes more than 360 million years ago. This transition from a strictly aquatic life to the capability of terrestrial existence marks a key evolutionary turning point for vertebrates. From these amphibian origins eventually came all other tetrapods—reptiles, birds and mammals.

The early amphibians diversified and remained the predominant terrestrial vertebrate group for nearly 100 million years. Although few details are known about the earliest ancestors of modern amphibian groups, the study of amphibian biology today is greatly enhanced when considered within the context of the important evolutionary transition these animals represent. A bi-phasic lifestyle, with aquatic larvae (often called tadpoles in the case of frogs) and primarily terrestrial adults, is a common developmental pattern for most present-day amphibians. Amphibian eggs are more similar in many ways to fish eggs than to the amniotic eggs of reptiles, birds and mammals, and cannot tolerate dry conditions. Most amphibian eggs are fertilized externally in water, where they will remain until hatching. However, other reproductive strategies have evolved

KLAUS O. RICHTER

Paedomorph Northwestern Salamander with freshly laid egg mass

that are less reliant on standing or flowing water. Some groups have evolved internal fertilization, some lay their eggs in moist terrestrial microhabitats where the embryos undergo direct development and bypass the larval stage, and in some species, the adults even carry the eggs or larvae with them to ensure that they don't dry out.

One of the major changes necessary for life on land was the development of respiratory structures that would function in air. Fish gills obviously do not work. Lungs were, and are, present in some fishes, but these structures became better developed in amphibians. However, lungs are not the only structures amphibians use to respire. During the aquatic larval stages, through which most amphibians pass, gills are used to acquire oxygen from the water. While amphibian gills function similarly, they are not derived directly from fish gills. In addition to larval gills and adult lungs, most amphibians also respire through capillary beds in their skin. Plethodontid salamanders have totally lost their lungs and

Pair of Oregon Spotted Frogs in amplexus

rely solely on cutaneous respiration. This is why the skin of almost all amphibians must remain moist, and why these creatures usually are associated with wet habitats.

The shift from water to land also required major changes associated with locomotion. Fish and early amphibian fossils clearly show the evolutionary changes in vertebral structure and the transition from fins to limbs that provided the foundation for all forms of tetrapod locomotion. Most salamanders have retained the ancestral locomotor anatomy and movement pattern—four limbs of roughly equal length and a reliance on lateral undulation both in water and on land. Frogs are wonderfully adapted for saltatory locomotion—jumping. Caecilians represent yet a third experimental form of locomotion seen also in snakes and some lizards—limblessness.

Ecosystems

Only recently have biologists begun to appreciate the ecological significance of amphibians. As more populations of frogs and salamanders are being studied, we are learning that amphibians play significant roles as predators and prey. In some ecosystems, the total biomass of amphibians is truly astounding and surely cannot be ignored in trying to understand ecological interactions and functions. The ultimate irony is that, just as we are learning about their role in ecosystems, these animals may be sounding a silent alarm about the quality of those environments. Since the mid-1980s, herpetologists have recognized that many amphibian populations have been in decline. Some entire species have gone extinct in a few short years.

Amphibians are far more than relics from another time. They inform us about the past, represent a significant portion of vertebrate diversity, play important biological roles in ecosystems, and may help us assess our future relationship with our environment. No doubt they are well worth learning about. Fascinating indeed!

Overview of Salamanders

Lynne Houck

Salamanders are a diverse group of amphibians. Although more closely related to frogs and toads, salamanders typically have the morphology of a lizard: four legs, a distinct trunk and a tail. Salamanders differ from lizards, of course, by having moist skin that lacks scales. There are ten families of living salamanders in the world and more than 475 species. The 30 salamander species found in northwestern North America are grouped into five families: mole salamanders, Pacific giant salamanders, torrent salamanders, newts and lungless salamanders.

Salamanders in northwestern North America exhibit the full range of life cycles, from completely aquatic to completely terrestrial (see table below). The oldest pattern is aquatic, meaning that animals live, mate and lay eggs in the water. A recent innovation (but one that is more than 70 million years old) is a life cycle that is completely terrestrial.

Aquatic-breeding salamanders vary in whether adults remain in the water permanently or migrate to terrestrial habitats after breeding. Migration may allow animals to avoid intense competition for food and to escape an ephemeral water source. For the salamander species which remain in water, adults usually retain certain larval features ("paedomorphism"), such as external gills, which facilitate their aquatic existence.

Salamander larvae have different morphological features depending on whether they develop in fast-flowing water (i.e., streams) or in water that is essentially

LIFE CYCLE	SALAMANDER SPECIES
Completely aquatic	Mole salamanders — Paedomorphic *Ambystoma gracile* and *A. tigrinum* Pacific giant salamanders—Paedomorphic *Dicamptodon*
Semi-aquatic	Torrent salamanders — *Rhyacotriton* spp.; adults occur in or near streams, splash zones from waterfalls, or seepages (occasionally are found in nearby wet forest)
Bi-phasic: terrestrial adults, larvae in lakes or ponds	Mole salamanders — *Ambystoma* spp.; larvae also found in slow-moving streams Newts: *Taricha* spp.; may also breed in slow-moving streams
Bi-phasic: terrestrial adults, larvae in streams	Pacific giant salamanders — Non-paedomorphic *Dicamptodon* spp.
Semi-terrestrial	Lungless salamanders — some plethodontids, especially *Plethodon dunni, P. vandykei, P. idahoensis*. Likely to occur in seepage areas, near waterfalls, and moist edges of streams
Completely terrestrial	Lungless salamanders — most plethodontids

Completely aquatic: both larvae and adults are permanently aquatic.

Semi-aquatic: larvae are aquatic; adults typically remain in or near water but occasionally can be found in the nearby forest.

Bi-phasic: larvae are aquatic; adults are terrestrial except for return to water during breeding season.

Semi-terrestrial: occurring in seeps and very shallow, flowing water.

Completely terrestrial: lacking any aquatic phase; eggs are laid on land, and larval development is completed within the egg.

Pair of Rough-skinned Newts in courtship

without currents (i.e., ponds and lakes). Salamander species that develop in fast-flowing water have dorsal fins that are reduced in height; they also have shorter gills. The larvae of species developing in ponds and lakes typically have dorsal fins of greater height, and they have longer gills. The variation in these morphological traits makes larval salamanders more hydrodynamically suited to their respective environments.

Terrestrial breeding is characteristic of the lungless salamanders (family Plethodontidae). These species mate and lay eggs only on land, never in ponds or streams. Clutches are laid in moist, protected sites, and each larval salamander develops completely within its egg. A terrestrial-breeding female guards her eggs until they hatch, which can take several months. When first hatched, a young lungless salamander looks like a miniature adult. Shortly after hatching, the female and her young go their own ways.

Salamander reproduction involves many other intriguing behaviors and physiological features. All Pacific Northwest salamanders have a two-step internal fertilization process. In the first step, the male inseminates the female by transferring sperm to her via a small structure termed a spermatophore. The spermatophore has a clear, gelatinous base topped by a whitish mass of sperm. The male deposits the spermatophore on the substrate, and the female obtains the sperm by moving over the spermatophore and lodging the sperm mass in her cloaca. The second step of internal fertilization occurs within the female when the sperm is united with the female's ova to achieve fertilization. The significance of this two-step process is that females of many species do not immediately use newly acquired sperm to fertilize their eggs. Female lungless salamanders, for example, can store sperm for weeks or even months, and the male typically is not present when the female finds a secluded spot to fertilize and lay her eggs.

Internal fertilization, with the potential for a delay to occur between mating and egg-laying, has significant consequences for salamander mating systems. A mating system describes the nature of interactions between males and females during the breeding season. Species of *Ambystoma*, for example, have an explosive mating system in the sense that mating occurs suddenly and is over very quickly. During this time, males compete with each other to fertilize a female, and many dozens of spermatophores may be deposited in front of a single receptive female. The female typically moves over the spermatophore area and obtains sperm from the spermatophores of several different males. The female may retain sperm for a few days before fertilization and oviposition occur. In contrast, courtship and insemination in the lungless salamanders can occur at any time during a period of several months. Also, courtship most often involves extensive interactions between a single male-female pair, sometimes lasting for as long as nine hours. A courtship most often is successfully completed with the male's deposit of a single spermatophore and the transfer of that single sperm mass into the female's cloaca. Due to the multi-month courtship period, a lungless salamander female may be inseminated on different occasions and

Clouded Salamander eggs

WILLIAM LEONARD

by several different males before laying her clutch of eggs.

Salamander skin has many functions related to the organism's reproduction, life cycle and physiological ecology. Skin glands secrete a protective layer of mucus. For most salamanders living on land, this layer helps protect an animal from losing too much water through its skin. Also, oxygen can more easily dissolve into moist skin and ultimately enter the circulatory system. This source of oxygen is particularly important for the lungless salamanders, which do not have lungs. Other secretions produced by the skin can help prevent a salamander from being eaten by predators. The Rough-skinned Newt, for example, has a potent toxin in its skin. Other species can produce annoying, glue-like secretions from their tails when harassed by a predator.

Many salamanders have skin glands that produce chemical signals (pheromones) for communication. Pheromones communicate a variety of information: species, sex, reproductive condition and territory boundaries. Pheromones are particularly important during the mating season. Female newts that are in breeding condition, for example, produce pheromones that attract the attention of male newts. Other reproductive pheromones are produced by glands that are located on the male's chin (for example, in species of *Plethodon*). The male delivers pheromone secretions from his chin gland by rubbing the gland secretions on the female during courtship; these make the female more likely to mate with that male.

Because these diverse skin functions are critical to the survival and reproduction of these delicate creatures, it is especially important to handle salamanders with care. The topical lotions and insect repellents that we often use and the relatively high temperatures of our hands can prove fatal to salamanders.

Overview of Frogs and Toads

Deanna H. Olson

"Never try to catch two frogs with one hand."
—Chinese proverb

"The frog does not run in the daytime for nothing."
—Nigerian proverb

"Where there are no swamps there are no frogs."
—German proverb

"The frog does not drink up the pond in which he lives."
—Native American proverb

Stories of frogs and toads enrich global cultures. They are symbols of concepts as diverse as prosperity and stoicism. This is not surprising, as frogs and toads are some of the most watchable wildlife worldwide and are known from all continents but Antarctica. They are members of the vertebrate order Anura (Latin for "without tail"). Of the almost 5,000 anuran species on Earth, 17 species are found in northwestern North America.

Compared to salamanders, frogs and toads have longer hind limbs, an external ear or tympanum and middle ear structures, and no tail. The distinction between "frogs" and "toads" is not scientific but rather is based loosely on stereotypes of two lifestyles common in the group. Frogs are more aquatic, with smooth and moist skin, webbed feet and long hind legs for swimming and jumping. In contrast, toads have characteristics more suited to a terrestrial life: they have a squat appearance, with warty and dry skin, poison (parotoid) glands behind their eyes, and relatively shorter hind legs for walking. Epitomizing these contrasting features are the "true toads" (genus *Bufo,* the group to which two of three toad species belong in the Pacific Northwest) and the "true frogs" (genus *Rana,* the genus to which ten of the fourteen frog species belong in our region).

Anurans have complex life histories that usually involve aquatic eggs and larvae (tadpoles) and semi-aquatic to terrestrial juveniles and adults. In the Northwest, breeding occurs in ephemeral and permanent water bodies, including both natural lakes and streams, and in more disturbed areas such as roadside ditches, flooded agricultural fields and backyard ponds. During breeding, males may be distinguished from females by their calls and vocal sacs at their throats, or by the development of nuptial pads on their thumbs, rough thickened skin that facilitates their clasping of females (amplexus). Frog and toad breeding can be "explosive" in that it may involve the synchronous aggregation of a local adult population. Such mating swarms may last for only a very limited time, hours to days. At the other extreme, breeding can be extended over a longer timeframe, wherein males may establish calling territories. A mating pair oviposits either a single egg clutch in a round mass or long string form, or several smaller egg clusters or packets. Clutch size varies with species, female size and sometimes locality (e.g., elevation gradients), from about 30 to 25,000 eggs.

Larvae hatch from eggs and are soon free-swimming. They may be found singly but often are found in schools, sometimes in very large numbers. An estimate of >1,000,000 Western Toad tadpoles have been observed schooling in a Cascade Range lake. Chemical communication among tadpoles in schools has been documented; for example, chemicals emitted during predation attempts can serve to warn nearby conspecifics of the potential threat. The time to metamorphosis may be only a month or two (Great Basin Spadefoot), about fifteen months (Bullfrog, which metamorphoses in August or September of the year after oviposition), or one to five years (tailed frogs.).

Juxtaposed between aquatic and terrestrial lifestyles, frogs and toads are central to food webs in both water and land. Tadpoles are omnivorous and, in turn, are prey for aquatic insects, fishes and some birds. With metamorphosis comes a diet change to carnivory. On land, frogs and toads become prey to additional birds and mammals. Cryptic coloration, skin toxins and nocturnal habits may be defenses against predators.

The general ecology of juveniles and adults varies with species. More terrestrial forms such as Pacific Treefrogs and Western Toads are routinely found distant from water bodies and have been reported using ground cover such as cracks, crevices, logs and rodent burrows. Spadefoots create their own burrows. Ranid frogs are often found along the banks of water bodies. Some species may have quite different breeding, foraging and overwintering habitats.

Several frogs in the Northwest have unique characteristics. Tailed frogs are considered the most primitive living frog, belonging to an ancestral lineage separate from all other frog and toad species. These frogs are distinct in that the males have a tail-like mating organ that allows them to inseminate females internally. Cascades Frog *(Rana cascadae)* tadpoles have highly attuned kin recognition abilities and prefer to aggregate with relatives rather than with non-relatives. They can distinguish between

Nuptial pad on the "thumb" of a male Northern Red-legged Frog

WILLIAM LEONARD

full siblings and both paternal and maternal half-siblings. Wood Frogs *(R. sylvatica)* are freeze-tolerant, a useful adaptation for these denizens of the far north of British Columbia. As winter brings subfreezing temperatures, water freezes into ice crystals within the bodies of these frogs without damaging their tissues, enabling them to hibernate until the spring thaw. Frogs and toads are known for their booming breeding choruses; these are signature events heralding the onset of spring in the temperate zone. At odds with this stereotype, a number of frogs and toads in the Northwest are either not vocal (tailed frogs) or not very audible (Western Toad, red-legged frogs, Oregon Spotted Frog and Cascades Frog). Finally, five species are unique to the Northwest: Cascades Frog, Oregon Spotted Frog, Northern Red-legged Frog, Coastal Tailed Frog and Rocky Mountain Tailed Frog.

Conservation of frogs and toads is an issue being addressed regionally as well as globally. In the Pacific Northwest, about 70% of anuran species have Status of Concern. A challenge in the Northwest is to identify potential threats, causes of losses and effective protections for frogs and toads in both their aquatic and terrestrial habitats. Furthermore, lack of basic understanding of current distributions and abundances, and population trends over time, has prompted the development of standard survey methods, and initiation of inventory and monitoring programs. Many regional lands, for example, are being censused, and electronic databases of amphibian localities are being maintained so that sites can be tracked into the future. It will take proactive efforts to keep our regional frogs and toads as watchable wildlife for everyone to continue to enjoy.

BIOGEOGRAPHIC PATTERNS

R. Bruce Bury and Gwendolynn W. Bury

Biogeography is a discipline that examines the distribution patterns and spatial relationships of biodiversity. Biogeography explores species relationships with habitats, geographic positions, precipitation patterns and temperature limits. It lets us better understand why certain species are present in an area.

The Pacific Northwest has a complex mosaic of landscapes and plant communities, reflecting steep gradients in mountain terrain and precipitation over short distances. Several distinct patterns of amphibian distributions (elements) are evident, mainly associated with large spatial areas (north, south, east, west) but also with different elevations in the same geographic location. We present four Northwest elements and describe one region of special interest where three elements overlap and that has its own unique species.

Widespread Element

Several species occupy large geographic expanses across all or most of the Pacific Northwest. Although occurring in a range of conditions, most of these species have specific requirements, such as ponds for breeding sites. This group includes the Long-toed Salamander, Rough-skinned Newt and, along the western edge of North America, the Ensatina salamander. Also belonging to this element are the Western Toad, Pacific Treefrog and the introduced Bullfrog—an invasive species from eastern North America.

Northern Element

This group lives in cool, wet forests from northwestern California to western British Columbia. It has 23 species and five families overall, with members of stream-, terrestrial- and pond-breeding assemblages. It includes all three of the endemic families associated with streams or seeps: torrent salamanders (Rhyacotritonidae), Pacific giant salamanders (Dicamptodontidae) and tailed frogs (Ascaphidae). It also includes many northern species of lungless salamanders (family Plethodontidae), most of which have restricted or geographically small distributions. They are associated with talus, rocky soils or downed wood in forested stands. In Washington, Van Dyke's Salamander frequents seeps and rocky talus in the Coast and Cascade Ranges. The Larch Mountain Salamander is found in the Columbia River Gorge and in patches of the Washington Cascade Mountains. Clouded, Dunn's and Western Red-backed Salamanders have relatively large ranges in the Northwest. The Oregon Slender Salamander occurs only in the northern portion of the Oregon Cascades, usually under large, coarse, woody material on the forest floor. There are also three true frogs (family Ranidae) in the region of the northern element, and all may be declining in numbers. Northern Red-legged Frogs occupy valleys and lowland forested areas throughout the region. Cascades Frogs occur only in montane ponds and lakes. The Oregon Spotted Frog once occurred in permanent waters in interior valleys but is now absent from most of its westernmost range. Oregon Spotted Frogs still are found in a few sites in the Cascade Range and Puget Trough.

Southern Element

The center of this group's range is in northern California and extends southward. These species are able to persist in somewhat drier, warmer conditions than the

WILLIAM LEONARD

Rainy Pass fen, Washington. Habitat for Western Toads, spotted frogs, Long-toed Salamanders

northern element. Southern habitats include deciduous-conifer woods, oak-woodlands, chaparral and rolling grassy foothills. This group includes about ten species, several of which are endemics with restricted range sizes, including: Red-bellied Newts that live only on the wet western slopes of the Coast Range in northern California; Wandering Salamanders that occur from the Smith River near the Oregon border to Mendocino County, mostly in dense forests; and in the interior, Shasta Salamanders that are restricted to limestone outcrops north of Shasta Lake.

There are increasing numbers of this group of amphibians south of the California-Oregon border. The Black Salamander ranges south to the Monterey Bay area, while the California Slender Salamander barely enters coastal Oregon but is widespread in California. The Arboreal Salamander occurs from about 100 km south of the Oregon border to Baja California Norte, and the California Newt ranges widely. Foothill Yellow-legged Frogs frequent edges of streams and rivers in warmer areas from southern Oregon to

Baja California. The California Red-legged Frog ranges from near the San Francisco Bay area southward; it is listed as a U.S. Federal Threatened Species. The California Giant Salamander lives in the San Francisco and Monterey Bay areas.

Eastern Element

Another 10 species of Pacific Northwest amphibians occur east of the Cascade Range and are broken into two main groups. First, there is a montane group with three species restricted to densely forested portions of the northern Rocky Mountains: the Rocky Mountain Tailed Frog, Coeur d'Alene Salamander and Idaho Giant Salamander. All of these likely dispersed to the Rockies in earlier times and evolved in isolation as separate species now distinct from counterparts farther west in the Cascades and other areas of the Northwest. The other group has species adapted to breed in ponds and wetlands in cold desert or plains ecosystems: Great Basin Spadefoot Toads and Columbia Spotted Frogs occur over much of the Great Basin. Several pond-breeding species in eastern Oregon and Washington extend from the central United States: the Northern Leopard Frog, Woodhouse's Toad, Tiger Salamander and Pacific Treefrog.

Klamath-Siskiyou Region

This region straddles the border between southwestern Oregon and northwestern California. It has the highest species diversity of amphibians in the Pacific Northwest because of an overlap between the northern and southern elements. Also, the region has two endemic species of lungless terrestrial salamander, the Del Norte Salamander and Siskiyou Mountains Salamander. The Scott Bar Salamander is a new species recently detected here from a limited area. This region has the north-south parallel alignment of the Coast and Cascade Ranges, and an east-west transecting topography of the Siskiyou Mountains. These features, in addition to the many river systems within them, likely served as both corridors and barriers, with pockets of refugia to allow animals to shift ranges and to persist during periods of environmental change in the past. The western slopes of the area experience maritime conditions of high precipitation and moderate temperatures, which are favored by many amphibians. These conditions add to the diversity of the regional herpetofauna.

Biogeography reflects species' adaptations. For example, cold-adapted species occur in forested mountain slopes and their fast-flowing, steep streams. Warm-adapted species live in openings in the forest canopy, on south-facing slopes, or in drier habitats such as oak woodland. These varied conditions are sometimes in close proximity to each other, adding to the diverse patterns and unique amphibian fauna of the Northwest.

Shallow marsh at Harts Pass, Washington

WILLIAM LEONARD

TAXONOMY AND GENETIC DIVERSITY

R. Steven Wagner

Taxonomy is the science of identifying and classifying different species based upon their evolutionary relationships. These relationships reflect the history of amphibians, and this history can be pieced together by examining their genes. Over the past several decades, many new molecular, genetic and biochemical methods have enabled us to delineate and categorize amphibians in new, more accurate ways. In addition to taxonomically defining species, our new understanding of amphibian populations is becoming increasingly important for their conservation and management. Basically, by using modern genetic techniques along with more traditional morphological studies, we are gaining a richer understanding of the natural history, population structure and dynamics, biogeography and conservation status of Pacific Northwest amphibians.

In the Pacific Northwest, molecular genetic studies have revealed several cryptic species, and family relationships have been reordered. The lineages in which new species have been identified include: (1) Pacific giant salamanders (Dicamptodontidae, two new species), torrent salamanders (Rhyacotritonidae, three new species), and tailed frogs (Ascaphidae, one new species), which are all endemic to stream habitats in Pacific Northwest mesic coniferous forests; (2) lungless salamanders (Plethodontidae, three new species and multiple distinct populations), which are forest-associated terrestrial species; and (3) true frogs (Ranidae, one new species) associated with lentic habitats.

In particular, a complex phylogenetic history is being unveiled within the plethodontid terrestrial salamanders. For example, genetic differences between Van Dyke's Salamander *(Plethodon vandykei)* and Coeur d'Alene Salamander *(Plethodon idahoensis)* suggest they warrant separate species designations, with *P. vandykei* occurring in the Coastal, Olympic and Cascade Ranges and *P. idahoensis* found in the interior.

Secondly, recent studies of the Clouded Salamanders, which are arboreal Pacific Northwest salamanders, suggest these plethodontids belong to an ancient, deep-branching lineage that is estimated to have diverged from the rest of the western Plethodontidae family of salamanders during the early Miocene. They have an interesting disjunct geographic distribution, being found in Oregon and northern California, and on Vancouver Island (British Columbia, Canada) but not in Washington. Genetic evidence from protein and mitochondrial DNA differences indicate that Oregon populations of salamanders (Clouded Salamanders, *Aneides ferreus)* should be considered a separate species from California populations (Wandering Salamanders, *Aneides vagrans)*, which last shared a common ancestor about 5 million years ago. There appears to be no genetic difference among Vancouver Island *Aneides* and California *Aneides*. This pattern of distribution provides a curious hypothesis concerning the introduction of Clouded Salamanders to Vancouver Island

Clouded Salamander late-stage embryos

during the late nineteenth century by being transported on shipments of Tanoak from California. Thus, the California and Vancouver Island salamanders were given the name "the Wandering Salamander (*A. vagrans*)" because of their presumed hitchhiking. The implication is that *A. vagrans* was introduced to and rapidly colonized Vancouver Island, which is remarkable considering that *A. ferreus* has not expanded into available habitat in Washington state.

Lastly, the distinction between the Del Norte Salamander (*Plethodon elongatus*) and the Siskiyou Mountains Salamander (*Plethodon stormi*) has always been controversial. However, recent mitochondrial DNA studies support the split and suggest that *P. stormi* is composed of two species, while *P. elongatus* consists of a complex of discrete populations.

Genetically divergent lineages within species have been identified in other plethodontid taxa. A genetic study among Larch Mountain Salamander (*Plethodon larselli*) populations occurring on opposite banks of the Columbia River revealed genetic differences accumulated from over 2 million years of isolation. Similarly, distinct lineages occur within Oregon Slender Salamander (*Batrachoseps wrighti*). These genetic differences are reflective of the low dispersal abilities of many plethodontids, which can become isolated over time by geographic barriers or geologic events. Many of these species are found in association only with mature forests; therefore, the recognition of within species genetic diversity can aid in their management and conservation.

The Spotted Frog (*Rana pretiosa*) has undergone an important taxonomic change that has implications for its conservation, too. The western populations have been designated as Oregon Spotted Frog (*Rana pretiosa*), and the eastern populations have been designated as the Columbia Spotted Frog (*Rana luteiventris*). Oregon Spotted Frogs have dramatically declined from much of their former range compared to

Pacific Treefrog metamorphs

WILLIAM LEONARD

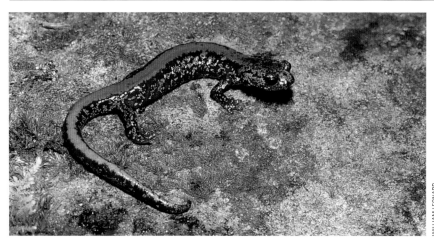

WILLIAM LEONARD

Coeur d'Alene Salamander

Columbia Spotted Frogs. Therefore, Oregon Spotted Frogs have been recently proposed for listing as an Endangered Species and can be managed independently of the Columbia Spotted Frog.

The taxonomic placement of the most well-recognized Pacific Northwest amphibian, the Pacific Treefrog, known for its loud, distinctive "rib-it, rib-it" call, has been controversial. Belonging to the treefrog family Hylidae, it was recognized initially as a New World treefrog, placed in the genus *Hyla* and designated as *Hyla regilla*. Several studies during the early part of the last decade suggested it was more closely aligned with members of the chorus frog genus *Pseudacris*. But more recent genetic evidence has suggested that the classic *Hyla* genus designation may be warranted after all. The two genera, *Hyla* and *Pseudacris,* appear to be closely related sister groups, making discrimination based on their relationships difficult; however, in the literature, most herpetologists refer to the species as *Hyla regilla*.

Similarly, controversy has lingered on the use of *Spea* or *Scaphiopus* for the genus designation of spadefoot toads. The genetic evidence suggests that Great Basin Spadefoots *(S. intermontana)* are a poly-phyletic group (composed of at least two different taxa), with the Rocky Mountain region spadefoots more closely related to *Scaphiopus bombifrons* than the Great Basin Spadefoots. However, more detailed population genetic studies are needed to tease apart these relationships so we can gain a greater understanding of the history of speciation in spadefoots.

For the average person and even for practicing herpetologists, the taxonomic changes taking place can be confusing and frustrating. However, as more information becomes available through morphological, ecological and genetic studies, we understand more about the rich history of these species. The recognition of distinct taxonomic groups, new species and the amount of genetic diversity within species can greatly aid in the conservation of the unique amphibians of the Pacific Northwest.

DECLINING AMPHIBIAN POPULATIONS

Andrew R. Blaustein

As part of an overall "biodiversity crisis" —an accelerated rate of species extinctions—many amphibian populations are declining throughout the world. Scientists first officially recognized the global loss of amphibian populations as a phenomenon worthy of worldwide attention in 1989. By 1993, more than 500 populations of frogs and salamanders were recognized as declining, and many species were listed as being of special conservation concern.

Numerous causes have been invoked to explain amphibian population declines. These include habitat destruction, climate change, increasing levels of ultraviolet radiation, environmental contamination, disease and the introduction of non-native species. Increasing evidence, however, suggests that many factors are responsible for amphibian population declines and that no single factor is causing all of the declines. Moreover, several factors may interact synergistically to adversely affect amphibian populations.

The Pacific Northwest has been a "hotbed" of activity with regard to amphibian population declines. Since the mid-1990s, numerous papers have been published documenting declining populations of amphibians in Oregon, Washington, northern California and adjacent states. Numerous papers have also been published concerning the factors contributing to amphibian population declines in the Pacific Northwest.

There is more information on declines in frog and toad populations compared with salamander populations. For example, in several regions of the Pacific Northwest, Northern Red-legged (*Rana aurora*) and Cascades (*R. cascadae*) Frogs as well as Western Toad (*Bufo boreas*) populations are in decline. However, populations of Pacific Treefrogs (*Pseudacris regilla*) appear to be robust. Due to a lack of good quantitative data, the status of the populations of most salamander species in the Pacific Northwest is unknown.

As in other regions, there are various factors contributing to the population declines of Pacific Northwest amphibian populations. Habitat destruction is a primary cause for the loss of amphibian populations in the Pacific Northwest. This includes logging, paving of wetlands and general human population growth that is expanding to rural counties. There is evidence that at least two pathogens are involved in amphibian mortality. These are the chytridiomycete, *Batrachochytrium dendrobatidis,* found in several areas of California where population declines have occurred, and a pathogenic oomycete,

Olympic Torrent Salamander larva

WILLIAM LEONARD

ROBERT M. STORM

Oregon Spotted Frog, Benton County, Oregon—the last known specimen from Willamette Valley

Saprolegnia ferax, contributing to large-scale embryonic mortality in Oregon, Washington and other regions of the Pacific Northwest. Increasing ultraviolet (UV) radiation appears to affect the embryos of several species of Northwest amphibians, including those of the red-legged and Cascades Frogs and Northwestern *(Ambystoma*

Northwestern Salamander

WILLIAM LEONARD

gracile) and Long-toed *(A. macrodactylum)* Salamanders. However, embryos of spotted frogs *(Rana pretiosa* and *R. luteiventris)* studied in Washington appear to be somewhat resistant to UV radiation, as are eggs of Pacific Treefrogs and those of red-legged frogs. Contaminants, including pesticides and nitrogen-based fertilizers, are also affecting amphibians in the Pacific Northwest. Introduced Bullfrogs *(Rana catesbeiana)* and fishes have also contributed to the declines of some amphibian populations. Non-native species may compete with and prey upon native amphibians. Moreover, they can introduce harmful pathogens to native amphibian populations.

Amphibians in the Pacific Northwest are being bombarded by a variety of agents that are detrimental to their populations. Because amphibians are such integral components of Pacific Northwest ecosystems, it is important that we accurately assess the status of their populations and attempt to alter the causes for their population declines.

HABITATS

Wetland Habitats

Klaus O. Richter

Wetlands (lentic or stillwater habitats) are among the most important habitats for Northwest amphibians. It is within the shallow, emergent vegetation zone of wetlands that almost all of our frogs and toads (except the tailed frogs) and several of our salamanders prefer to breed and lay their eggs, and where their larvae forage for food and seek cover. Thus, wetlands may be the exclusive habitat within which amphibian eggs develop, with the resulting larvae growing for one to several years prior to metamorphosis and life on land. For paedomorphic salamanders, wetlands remain their sole life-long habitat. Moreover, the wetland ecotone—the wetted edge and riparian transition zone between wetlands and drier uplands—is the unique habitat in which newly metamorphosed frogs and salamanders occur and feed during dry summer periods prior to cooler and wetter fall conditions. Wetland edges are also where the adults of numerous amphibian species spend much of their lives. The moist soil, dense vegetation and other favorable microclimatic conditions adjoining wetland edges also minimize the potential for desiccation and provide cover from predators, while simultaneously providing abundant insect, spider and other invertebrate foods.

Wetlands are lentic habitats that encompass virtually all types of shallow water bodies characterized by slow or quiescent currents, deep organic soils and hydrophytes—the unique plants that tolerate seasonal or intermittent flooding every other year or so on average. Not surprisingly, some wetlands may not have all three of these conditions. The playa wetlands and vernal pools, found in drier climates east of the Cascades and extending from northern California to British Columbia, may lack deep organic soils.

Since childhood, we have referred to wetlands by names such as marsh, swamp, bog and even fen. Marshes are flooded or saturated areas in which rooted, water-tolerant, soft-stemmed vegetation dominates, including grasses, sedges, rushes and other herbaceous plants. Swamps are characterized by somewhat less flooded wet areas, dominated by woody shrubs and trees. Bogs are topographic depressions with virtually no drainage, characterized by acidic water, low nutrients, Sphagnum "peat" mosses and uniquely acid-tolerant plants. In contrast, water flowing through fens is less acidic and more nutrient rich; consequently these systems are dominated by sedges, grasses and shrubs.

Amphibians, however, are associated with a wide variety of other natural and anthropogenic wetland areas, including shallow lakeshore edges, floodplains, oxbows, river embayments and riparian fringes of shallow water along streams. Some amphibians are most often found in temporarily flooded wetlands, including vernal pools, playas, springs, seeps, swales and other moist areas. Some amphibians are found in unexpected habitats, such as farm sloughs, roadside ditches and other flooded areas that provide water and some vegetation characteristics similar to wetlands. Often these areas are used because they are the only remaining wet environment in the landscape. Generally, amphibians are not found in estuarine wetlands, although they may occasionally be found feeding in the nearshore environment and somewhat regularly in wetlands of coastal dunes.

The colloquial terms describing wetlands (marshes, swamps, bogs, fens, etc.) were formalized by scientists into a standardized, widely accepted scientific terminology with specific ecological, regulatory and legal usage. Consequently, wetlands are also known by specific technical terms describing their hydrology, vegetation and substrate conditions and, hence, more cumbersome names. For example, a Palustrine, semi-permanently flooded, emergent wetland with an unconsolidated bottom is essentially a pond-like wetland that dries out every other year or so on average, and is further characterized by herbaceous plants in shallow areas in which the bottom consists of sand or mud, not gravel or rock. In another classification system, wetlands are named primarily by their geomorphic setting and hydrology. For example, wetlands that owe their characteristics to stream conditions are identified as riparian wetlands, whereas others with no outflow or inflow other than from precipitation are called depressional wetlands.

Regardless of terminology, wetlands are recognized as dynamic areas in which the characteristics of water, soil moisture and vegetation often change seasonally and/or yearly. Yet these systems retain their overall condition unless dramatically influenced by wildlife (beaver dams) or humans (farmers draining, ranchers grazing, developers channeling runoff). They are found throughout the Pacific Northwest in coastal backwater dunes, floodplain and river deltas, dense old-growth forests, open oak savannas, Ponderosa Pine stands, deserts (i.e., sagebrush areas and playa wetlands), and in alpine and subalpine meadows. Indeed, these systems are found wherever temperature, precipitation and other aspects of climate encourage both the flooding and vegetation characteristic of wetlands and their amphibian assemblage. Interestingly, west-slope, low-elevation, seasonal wetlands often have the highest diversity and number of amphibians because of an absence of fish and a diminished number of invertebrate predators. Therefore, such wetlands

Lake Evan, Snohomish County, Washington

WILLIAM LEONARD

may have large numbers of each species, including Pacific Treefrogs, red-legged frogs and Long-toed Salamanders.

A general misconception of amphibian ecology in the Pacific Northwest is that amphibians are permanent residents of wetlands, and that they spend their entire lives at ponds, lake margins and other wetlands. Hence, people often fail to recognize the critical importance of adjacent upland habitat. It is the combination of wetland breeding areas and adjacent upland forests, woodlots and meadow living areas that are critical for amphibian survival. With the exception of mountain populations, many of our native wetland amphibians only breed in wetlands over a period of a few weeks. Thereafter, they return to adjacent vegetated communities for the rest of the year to feed, hibernate and carry out all other life activities. Clearly, wetlands are critical to pond-breeding amphibians, and pond hydrology and water quality are important to ongoing amphibian usage. This has led wetland ecologists to seriously consider amphibian species, abundance and health at a wetland as an indicator of the overall health of that wetland.

Stream, Near-stream and Seepage Habitats

Lawrence L.C. Jones

The amphibian fauna of the Northwest is particularly noteworthy because of the number of species associated with lotic (flowing) water habitats. This includes three endemic families: torrent salamanders (family Rhyacotritonidae, four species); Pacific giant salamanders (Dicamptodontidae, four species); and tailed frogs (Ascaphidae, two species). There are also a number of species of lungless salamanders (Plethodontidae) associated with streams, although none of them have aquatic larvae, as do some plethodontids from eastern North America. From northwestern California to Washington, west-side streams often have the full complement of three species of stream-dwelling amphibians (a torrent salamander, a Pacific giant salamander and a tailed frog, depending on geographic area). Inland areas have one or two (a tailed frog and/or a Pacific giant salamander), while northwestern Oregon, southwestern Washington and some areas of the Cascades have four species (because Cope's and Coastal Giant Salamanders often co-occur). All of our stream-dwelling amphibians are supremely adapted to life in cold, turbulent streams or their margins.

The climate of the Northwest is ideal for the formation of seepages ("seeps") and streams that can support amphibians. Moisture-laden clouds from the cold North Pacific currents enter the North American mainland, from Alaska to northwestern California, dumping large amounts of precipitation for much of the year. The western slopes of coastal mountains receive most of the rain, while the eastern slopes and basins are in a "rain shadow" and receive far less rainfall. Thus, most of the stream-associated amphibians are on the west slopes of the coastal ranges and

Cascade Mountains. Along the coast, there is a relatively mild, maritime climate, where precipitation and humidity are high and freezing temperatures are rare, giving amphibians an extended period when they can be surface active. Inland areas and those at higher elevations often have freezing temperatures, with large amounts of snowfall. Stream amphibians have a smaller window of activity in these habitats and must be able to endure these hardships. It is amazing how adaptable these animals can be. For example, tailed frogs may be found above timberline, a seemingly harsh environment for an ectothermic animal. Northwestern stream-associated amphibians are among the most cold-tolerant, desiccation-prone amphibians in the world.

By following a stream from its origin, we can observe how different taxa use the lotic environments differently. As moisture fills the water table in the mountains, it flows out of the surface at places known as seeps. Seeps usually have little flow, so they do not form a channel. Water in seeps is basically a thin film that flows between and under rocks and wood. This is the realm of the torrent salamanders, although they may be found in deeper waters and on land near the stream. Occasionally, some of the stream-associated plethodontids are found in seeps also. As water flows downhill, the volume increases, erosion increases and streams are formed. The most productive streams (for amphibians) tend to be those that are between 1 and 3 meters wide, rocky and somewhat steep. Mountain streams tend to have what is called a step-pool form, which means that pools are separated by riffles (fast water) and cascades (plunging water). Step pools are formed by gravity, water flow and deposition of logs and rocks. In the pools, we tend to find Pacific giant salamanders, while in the riffles and cascades, we tend to find tailed frogs.

WILLIAM LEONARD

Trestle Creek, Bonner County, Idaho

The edges of streams and splash zones of cascades and waterfalls are often seep-like habitats, so that is the best area to find torrent salamanders in larger streams, as well as in seeps that flow into the stream.

All species of stream-associated amphibians tend to be associated with rocks in the stream, but not all stream-associated amphibians are found in streams or seeps. Some are terrestrial but take advantage of the microclimate of the near-stream habitat. The near-stream environment is humid and buffers temperature extremes, ideal conditions for many species. Adults of all species with aquatic larvae and some plethodontids fall into this category.

As streams form over time, the hillsides erode away, forming a gorge outside the stream channel. Also, periodic flood events during the high water periods (fall through spring) help define the channel and gorge. Inside the gorge walls, we can find a number of other microhabitats, including floodplains, terraces and colluvial debris (rocks and logs that are eroding from, or above, the gorge). Some of the plethodontid salamanders of the near-stream realm include Van Dyke's, Dunn's, Coeur d'Alene and Black Salamanders. These species may be in seeps or splash zones, or within a few meters of a stream. Some salamanders, such as the Black Salamander and Western Red-backed Salamander, have geographic variation in their habitat relationships and are associated with streams only in parts of their range. Some frogs and toads may also take advantage of the streamside microclimate but tend not to be very closely associated with streams, as are these plethodontids.

As a group, stream-associated amphibians are considered indicators of stream and streamside health, particularly with regard to forest management. This is primarily because they are very sensitive to their surroundings, having evolved for thousands of years in cold mountain streams. Some of the potential threats to stream-dwellers following timber harvest or other activities include increased stream temperature, decreased oxygen and excessive siltation. These problems tend to be most pronounced on low-gradient streams where summer temperatures can be high. Hence, low-gradient streams in northwestern California or southwestern Oregon are intrinsically more at risk than high-gradient streams in the Cascades. In these examples, the streams in southern latitudes with a low-gradient stream will be silty, plus the high daytime temperatures may be fatal to stream-dwellers. Also, the increased temperature and decreased flow are synergistic, causing decreased oxygenation. However, a steep Cascades stream will flush silt downslope, and temperatures (and hence oxygenation) may be little changed following a disturbance. It should be noted, however, that this is a simplification, and each stream has its own set of environmental parameters.

Terrestrial Habitats
Richard S. Nauman and Kristiina Ovaska

Most of our amphibians rely on terrestrial habitats to some degree. Woodland salamanders complete their entire life-cycle, from egg to adult, on land. In our region, adults and juveniles of most aquatic-breeding salamanders and frogs forage in terrestrial habitats, and several overwinter on land. Often, dispersal from natal water bodies and migrations to and from breeding sites take place over land.

Some species, such as the tailed frogs, tend to remain close to water-courses throughout the year. Others, such as the Western Toad, may wander surprisingly far from water and can be found in upland areas many miles from water bodies. Chorus frogs and some salamanders are adapted to climbing. The champion tree-climber in our area is the Wandering Salamander, which has been found up to 90 m above ground on moss-covered branches of redwood trees. At the other end of the spectrum, mole salamanders spend much of their adult life in subterranean burrows.

Often the presence of amphibians is associated with key habitat features, which ameliorate fluctuations in temperature and moisture and enable amphibians to survive in a wide range of terrestrial habitats. These features include decaying wood, such as fallen logs, snags and piles of loose bark, and rocks, particularly talus. The three-dimensional habitat created by decaying wood and talus provides shelter and allows amphibians to select suitable moisture and temperature conditions.

Because amphibians derive their body heat from the environment and have a skin that is permeable to water, climatic conditions play a key role in their distribution in terrestrial habitats. Both long, cold winters and hot, dry summers limit the number of terrestrial species found in many areas. The following broad areas contain distinct terrestrial habitats and amphibian faunas:

Coastal, Temperate Rainforests
The wet coniferous and mixed forests that cover an extensive area between the Pacific Ocean and the crest of the Cascade Mountains hold the highest diversity of amphibians in the Pacific Northwest. The area is characterized by mild maritime climate, and stands of giant coniferous trees may be present. Moist, cool conditions under the shade of the forest canopy provide ideal habitat for terrestrial amphibians. Many species of woodland salamanders inhabit the forest floor and find shelter under the deep moss-mats and decaying logs. Other amphibians typical to these forests include the Coastal Giant Salamander, Cascade Torrent Salamander, Northwestern Salamander, Rough-skinned Newt, Coastal Tailed Frog, red-legged frogs and Western Toad.

Interior Forests
Wet coniferous and mixed forests also occur farther east along the western Rocky Mountains. The climate is harsh, characterized by short summers and cold winters. Species that spend much of their adult life in terrestrial environments but migrate to ponds to breed soon after snow melt are widespread in this region and include the Long-toed Salamander, Pacific Treefrog and Western Toad. Other species, including the Columbia Spotted Frog and Northern Leopard Frog, occur in aquatic or marshland habitats but can be found in terrestrial habitats in moist woodlands. The single woodland salamander, the Coeur d'Alene Salamander, occupies terrestrial habitats near seepages and other wet areas.

Western Valleys and Coastal Lowlands
Low-elevation woodlands and grasslands from southwestern British Columbia to

near Eugene, Oregon (Puget Trough and Willamette Valley), flood seasonally, providing breeding habitat for a range of aquatic-breeding species, including the Rough-skinned Newt, Long-toed Salamander, Pacific Treefrog and Northern Red-legged Frog. After the breeding season, the adults of these species disperse and spend the remainder of the year in terrestrial habitats, retreating to rodent burrows and other shelters during dry periods in the summer. Species more typical of coastal or wet interior forests, such as the Western Red-backed Salamander, are found around forested margins of the valley but seem to be limited on the valley floors by the distribution of alluvial (river-deposited) soils. Much of this region has been impacted by agricultural and urban development. Some species, however, such as the Pacific Treefrog, the Long-toed Salamander and the Clouded Salamander, can tolerate some degree of disturbance and may be found in backyards and city parks.

Terrestrial habitat, Shasta County, California

WILLIAM LEONARD

Oak Woodlands

Oak woodlands are a common habitat in southern Oregon and northern California and provide suitable environments for a variety of lungless salamanders, including the Black Salamander, Arboreal Salamander, California Slender Salamander and Ensatina. In addition, terrestrial adults of aquatic-breeding species, such as newts and the Pacific Treefrog, can be common in these habitats.

Shrub-Steppe

Expansive areas of shrub-steppe dominate the Great Basin east of the Cascade Mountains. These areas provide limited habitat for all but the most drought-tolerant amphibians. Amphibians found in shrub-steppe habitats are typically adult forms of aquatic breeding species such as the Pacific Treefrog, Long-toed Salamander, Tiger Salamander

and Great Basin Spadefoot Toad. Adults of these species are often difficult to detect in terrestrial habitats except during their migrations to and from breeding sites. During the long summer drought, they seek refuge in rodent burrows or other underground retreats.

High-elevation Areas

Long winters with subzero temperatures and short, dry summers are characteristic of the higher elevations of the major mountain ranges of our region. Typically, all amphibians inhabiting high areas from forest habitats to glaciers and snowfields are aquatic-breeding species. Species such as the Cascades Frog, Pacific Treefrog, Columbia Spotted Frog (in Washington, Idaho and Montana), Western Toad and Long-toed Salamander use high-elevation terrestrial habitats for migration to and from the breeding sites and for foraging when moisture and thermal conditions are suitable. While abundant at lower elevations, plethodontid salamanders are usually absent from high-elevation areas (above 1500 m in northern California and southern Oregon and above 800 m in the more northern portion of the region).

Notes:

Diagrams:

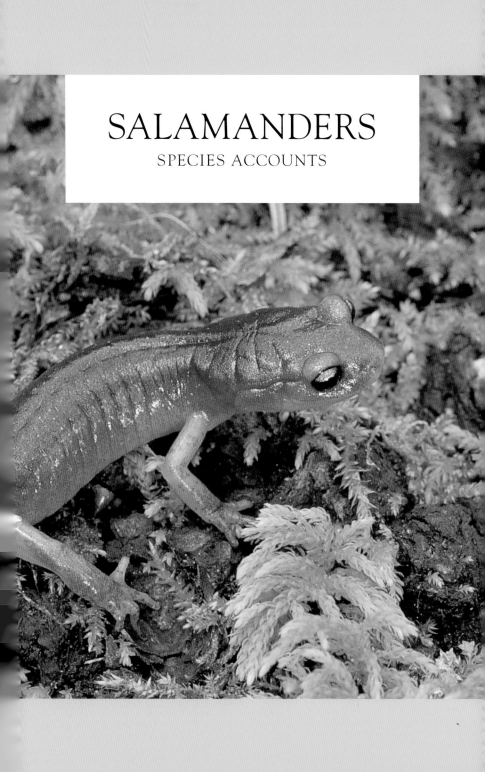

SALAMANDERS

SPECIES ACCOUNTS

NORTHWESTERN SALAMANDER

Ambystoma gracile   BAIRD

Author: Klaus O. Richter

Description: Northwestern Salamander adults occur as both non-gilled terrestrial forms and paedomorphic forms. Terrestrial adults and juveniles are **stocky and brown, with prominent, dark brown, protruding eyes** and relatively short, muscular limbs. Recently metamorphosed Northwestern Salamanders have features similar to adults, although their body shapes are thinner. Parotoid glands are present on the head, and poison glands occur on the sides of the tail. Adult length varies between 140–220 mm TL. The male's tail is slightly longer than half the TL, whereas the female's tail may be almost as long as the body length. Typical **paedomorphs have large, feathery, external gills** attached at the base on either side of the head. **Paedomorphic**

forms reach a body size similar to that of terrestrial forms. Their color ranges from brown to tan or olive-green. When viewed from above, the paedomorphic form has a small, somewhat rectangular or slightly hourglass-shaped head that gradually but distinctly slopes toward the snout. The legs (particularly the hind limbs) are short and are slightly wider than those of a non-gilled adult, presumably to aid in locomotion in the aquatic environment.

Variation: Unique color phases, including entirely black individuals and dark brown populations with white or yellowish flecking, exist in British Columbia and the Olympic Mountains. Gray-brown individuals occur in southeastern Alaska.

Eggs and Larvae: Initially, oviposited egg masses measure about 44 mm long by 27 mm wide. With time, they enlarge to a roundish, thick, firm, gelatinous mass measuring up to 85 mm long by 73 mm wide. They are most often found attached to vegetation or branches and other aquatic substrates in lentic habitats. An egg mass has 50–200 white to cream-colored eggs measuring 2.0–2.5 mm in diameter, each enclosed within a clear membrane measuring 5.5 mm in diameter. In a few days, eggs become tan or light brown in color. Within a week, some of the individual eggs take on a green color from photosynthetic algae that are presumed to be symbiotic. Prior to hatching, eggs may float in the water after separating from the attachment site. Hatchlings are approximately 8 mm TL, with a broad head twice the width of the body, a pair of small, hair-like balancers between the eyes, and a pair of gills, each with three long, feathery gill stalks aligned in a row. Larvae are usually dark, often with mottling along the tail set on a cream, dark gray or translucent background color. Larvae maintain their mottling and may have large, light, dorsal blotches on a darker background and a

Gravid female

*Thurston County,
Washington*

**Immature exhibiting
defensive posture**

*King County,
Washington*

Adult

*Thurston County,
Washington*

Adult female underwater with spermatophores
Mason County, Washington

Egg mass
Thurston County, Washington

First-year larva
King County, Washington

whitish to cream venter, often yellow or gold. Smaller larvae lack parotoid, tail and other granular skin glands, although these appear on older (50 mm TL), second-year larvae. Larvae do not have the protruding eyes or dark color of terrestrial adults.

Similar Species: Transformed Pacific giant salamanders lack prominent parotoid glands and usually have some marbling on the head. Long-toed Salamander larvae are difficult to distinguish from Northwestern Salamander larvae of similar age without considerable experience and careful viewing with a compound microscope or hand lens. Even then, identification may not be positive until confirmed upon transformation. Larval and paedomorphic Pacific giant salamanders have a greatly reduced tail fin. They also have short, bushy or filamentous gills and a "dog-faced" appearance when viewed laterally.

Distribution: Northwestern Salamanders are found primarily west of the Cascade Crest from northern California through British Columbia to extreme southeastern Alaska. In Washington, they also occur on the east slope of the Cascade Range near mountain passes and along the Columbia River.

Life History: Northwestern Salamanders breed from November to July, depending on weather, latitude and altitude, with earliest breeding during warm winters in the southern part of the range and at lowest altitudes. In the center of their range in lowland Oregon and Washington, breeding generally starts in mid-February and extends through mid-March. Eggs hatch in 2–4 weeks, depending on water temperature. While metamorphosis can occur in the fall of the first year, most individuals are believed to transform after at least one full year in the larval form.

Natural History: There can be synchrony in egg-laying at a site, and numerous egg masses can be found when conditions are favorable. These conditions include the presence of thin-stemmed, emergent plants in sunny locations at 30–60 cm water depths. Given choices in water depth, females deposit eggs about 5–20 cm below the surface. Terrestrial adults usually remain within 1 km of breeding sites, whereas dispersing juveniles may be found farther away from their natal wetlands. From fall through early summer, terrestrial forms are active at or just below the surface. They are most often found in the open during late winter and spring breeding migrations, but they will retreat below ground down root channels, small mammal burrows, crevices and holes. They may also dig into the soft litter and duff on the forest floor. Little is known about their subterranean existence. Both larval and terrestrial forms prey on amphibian larvae and terrestrial and aquatic invertebrates. In turn, predators—including dragonfly larvae, predaceous diving beetles, fish, Bullfrogs, gartersnakes, turtles, herons, Mink and Raccoons—readily eat Northwestern Salamanders. However, when disturbed, transformed adults exude a milky, noxious cream that quickly becomes tacky to the touch and presumably is unpalatable to predators.

Habitat: Northwestern Salamanders are found in mixed coniferous and deciduous forests. Cool, moist, complex forests may provide the ideal microclimate, enabling Northwestern Salamanders to feed on invertebrates both on the ground surface and under vegetation in litter, duff and other organic debris. Downed trees and branches constitute an essential habitat component for cover. Northwestern Salamanders breed in lentic environments, including lakes, ponds, wetlands, bays of rivers and streams, and in agricultural ditches and other man-made channels or potholes wherever current velocities are low or absent.

LONG-TOED SALAMANDER

Ambystoma macrodactylum　　　BAIRD

Author: Evelyn L. Bull

Description: The Long-toed Salamander is named for the **long fourth toe on its hind foot.** It has prominent costal grooves and smooth, black or dark gray skin with a dorsal stripe running from the head almost to the tip of the tail. The stripe may be solid, blotchy or absent. **Stripe color varies from gold, yellow or green to tan.** The sides, abdomen and chest usually have white or silver flecking on a gray or black surface. Adults measure to about 85 mm SVL and 165 mm TL.

　　Variation: Several subspecies can be found within the range of this field guide. These subspecies are most easily distinguished by their geographic distribution. The Western Long-toed Salamander *(A. m. macrodactylum)* is found west of the Cascade Range. The Eastern Long-toed Salamander *(A. m. columbianum)* is found east of the Cascade Range. The Southern Long-toed Salamander *(A. m. sigillatum)* occurs in southwestern Oregon. The Northern Long-toed Salamander *(A. m. krausei)* occurs in the Bitterroot Mountains in eastern Idaho, throughout western Montana, and north through western Alberta and eastern British Columbia to Jasper National Park. A fifth subspecies, the Santa Cruz Long-toed Salamander *(A. m. croceum),* occurs in Santa Cruz, California.

　　Eggs and Larvae: Eggs are about 2.0–2.5 mm in diameter with a soft, jelly coat surrounding them and have dark dorsal and white ventral poles. The outer envelopes of eggs may adhere to each other but are individually distinct. Females may deposit 85–411 eggs, usually in clusters of 10–30 eggs or sometimes singly. Larvae measure 10–13 mm TL at hatching and typically are brown or tan in color. The eyes are set in from the margin of the head. Prior to developing front limbs, the larvae have a pair of balancers protruding from the sides of the head. Sizes at metamorphosis range from 32–47 mm SVL.

　　Similar Species: Dunn's Salamander, Western Red-backed Salamander, Coeur d'Alene Salamander, Van Dyke's Salamander and Larch Mountain Salamander also may have yellow or greenish yellow dorsal stripes, but they have nasolabial grooves and short toes. Northwestern Salamander larvae are difficult to distinguish from Long-toed Salamander larvae but may sometimes show the beginnings of parotoid glands and glandular areas along the base of the dorsal fin. Rough-skinned Newt larvae have eyes at the outer margin of the head.

　　Distribution: Long-toed Salamanders have a broad range, extending from south-eastern Alaska to northern California and from the Pacific coast to north-central

Adult

*Trinity County,
California*

Adult

*Skamania County,
Washington*

Adult female

*Grant County,
Washington*

Egg mass
*Grant County,
Washington*

Egg mass
*Thurston County,
Washington*

Larva
*King County,
Washington*

Idaho, western Montana and western Alberta. They occur from sea level to about 2470 m in the Eagle Cap Wilderness (Wallowa County, Oregon) and over 2700 m in Idaho and Montana.

Life History: Long-toed Salamanders breed in winter when temperatures are above freezing. At warmer, low-elevation sites, breeding may begin as early as January, often following precipitation events. In cold, alpine environments, breeding can be as late as July after snowmelt. Eggs hatch in 2–5 weeks, depending on water temperature. Larvae metamorphose in the first summer in warm water at low elevations but require 2–3 years in colder water at higher elevations. In some localities, the amount of rainfall and hence water depths determine the length of time available for larval growth and thus the size at metamorphosis. Sexual maturity is reached at 2 years of age, with adult size reached at 3 years. Life span can be as long as 10 years, based on skeletal aging.

Natural History: Each year, adults migrate nocturnally to breeding ponds. Males arrive earlier and stay longer than females. Males deposit spermatophores that females pick up with their cloacae after courtship. Eggs are deposited singly or in loose clumps on the substrate, or they may be attached to vegetation or detritus underwater. Eggs may be deposited in shallow water (< 20 cm) or in deeper water (75 cm deep), where they are attached to vegetation or coarse, woody debris. Females leave the breeding pond soon after eggs are deposited. Predators of larvae include dragonfly larvae, predaceous diving beetles, gartersnakes, fish, kingfishers and wading birds. Gartersnakes, Bullfrogs, fish and herons may prey on adults. Long-toed Salamander adults prey upon woodlice, crickets, beetles, centipedes, earthworms and spiders. Larvae feed on zooplankton and small macroinvertebrates, including immature insects, crustaceans, snails, tadpoles and leeches.

Habitat: This species occurs in a variety of habitats, including forests, sagebrush communities and alpine meadows. Adults are primarily subterranean, but they can be found occasionally on the ground under bark, rocks or rotting wood. During breeding, adults are found in temporary or permanent ponds or in the shallow, quiet water at the edges of lakes and streams.

Remarks: Declines in this salamander have been observed, and several causal factors are implicated. The introduction of fish has caused losses due to predation on both adults and larvae. The density of larval Long-toed Salamanders is lower in sites with fish, compared to fishless sites in Idaho and most likely in other locations. Salamanders re-colonized high-elevation lakes after the extirpation of introduced trout in Montana. Declines of salamanders also have been linked to roadway mortality. For example, when roads in Waterton Lakes National Park in Alberta, Canada, intersected the terrestrial and aquatic habitats used by this species, the species declined. Eggs exposed to natural levels of UV-B radiation show increased mortality and a higher incidence of deformities than those shielded from this radiation. Finally, timber harvest may have adverse effects on this species: Long-toed Salamanders were found to be three times more abundant in unlogged sites than in logged sites in Montana.

TIGER SALAMANDER

Ambystoma tigrinum   GREEN

Author: Lisa A. Hallock

Description: The Tiger Salamander is a **large, stocky salamander with blotches.** Adults are 75–162 mm SVL **with a broad, rounded snout, small, protruding eyes and distinct costal grooves. The overall color is dark with olive, green or yellow blotches.** The blotches may be scattered over the entire body or may occur primarily on the dorsolateral surface. There are paired tubercles on the undersides of the feet. Mature males have swollen cloacae and laterally compressed tails during the breeding season. Paedomorphic forms grow to impressive sizes of up to 175 mm SVL. They are greenish in color and have large heads with huge gills, well-developed legs and wide toes.

Variation: The Tiger Salamander has six recognized subspecies. The primary

subspecies found in the Pacific Northwest is the Blotched Tiger Salamander *(A. t. melanostictum)*. The Arizona Tiger Salamander *(A. t. nebulosum)* occurs in this region only in the southeastern corner of Idaho. It differs in being olive-green to dark grayish above with scattered, small black dots on the dorsal surface and a lighter-colored belly mottled with dark markings.

Eggs and Larvae: The eggs are small, with an ovum and gelatinous envelope together measuring less than 10 mm in diameter. The ovum is grayish or brownish above and cream below. The eggs are laid singly or in small clusters on thin stems and twigs. Larvae are pond type with large, bushy gills and a broad dorsal fin. Hatchlings are approximately 15 mm TL and lack balancers. Small larvae are olive to greenish above with black or brown mottling and have a large, wide head and long gills. Larger larvae have an overall greenish coloration with or without dorsal spotting. Larvae are capable of transforming in the fall of their first year at approximately 75–125 mm TL, but metamorphosis also may be delayed until larvae are larger or, in the case of paedomorphic individuals, delayed indefinitely.

Similar Species: The adult Long-toed Salamander is less stocky and has a yellow, olive-green or tan dorsal stripe (which may be broken up into blotches), white or silver speckling on the sides of the body, thin toes, and a fourth hind toe that is distinctly longer than the other toes. Long-toed Salamander eggs are larger, with an ovum and gelatinous envelope measuring 10 mm or greater in diameter. Long-toed Salamander hatchlings have obvious balancers.

Distribution: The Tiger Salamander is the most widely distributed salamander in North America. Populations occur in central Canada, are scattered throughout much of the United States and extend south

Adult
*Douglas County,
Washington*

Adult
*Grant County,
Washington*

**Adult in
defensive posture**
*Douglas County,
Washington*

Paedomorph
*Grant County,
Washington*

WILLIAM LEONARD

Eggs and hatchling
*Grant County,
Washington*

WILLIAM LEONARD

**Portrait of a
first-year larva**
*Whitman County,
Washington*

WILLIAM LEONARD

into northern Mexico. Tiger Salamander larvae are widely used as fishing bait and, as a consequence, have been introduced to many areas. In our region, Tiger Salamanders occur from south-central British Columbia to the Columbia Plateau of eastern Washington and western Idaho. Isolated occurrences are also known from the Colville area and south-central Klickitat County in Washington. Locations in Oregon are patchy, with confirmed reports for The Dalles area, the Klamath Falls vicinity and the Moon Reservoir in Harney County. In northern California, populations occur in Siskiyou County. Populations in Oregon and California may have been introduced.

Life History: Breeding takes place from March to May in permanent and semi-permanent water bodies without predatory fish. The incubation period for the eggs is approximately 2–4 weeks but varies depending on temperature and pond conditions. Larval forms can be abundant in some areas and may be represented by many age and size classes. Growth rate, timing of metamorphosis and size at metamorphosis vary geographically and are influenced by environmental factors such as water temperature, pond duration, larval density and food availability. Environmental factors, as well as genetic factors, influence the development of paedomorphic adults and cannibalistic morphs. In the Pacific Northwest, metamorphosis most often occurs after the second year. Tiger Salamanders are a long-lived species. The lifespan of some individuals in captivity has exceeded 16 years.

Natural History: The terrestrial forms are nocturnal and spend the majority of their lives in subterranean burrows. They are rarely seen except occasionally on spring nights as they migrate to and from breeding ponds. These migrations are apparently triggered by rain when temperatures are above freezing. Small

larvae eat zooplankton. Larger larvae eat a variety of aquatic organisms, including worms, insects and other invertebrates, mollusks, and amphibian eggs and larvae. Cannibalistic forms occur under certain conditions. Little is known about the diet of the terrestrial forms, although insects, worms, small field mice, snails and small snakes have been reported. Mass mortality of the larval forms occurs in some years due to pond drying. Major die-offs of diseased salamanders have been reported from some populations in the Northwest.

Habitat: In the Northwest, the Tiger Salamander inhabits grasslands, shrub-steppe and open forests in areas that have water bodies without predatory fish. Tiger Salamanders excavate their own burrows. They also use mammal burrows and tunnel systems.

Remarks: The California Tiger Salamander (*A. californiense*) is a closely related taxon that, until recently, was considered a subspecies of the Tiger Salamander, but most authorities currently recognize this species as valid. The two species are similar in appearance, but *A. californiense* typically has a pattern that is more spotted than barred. California Tiger Salamanders are found in low-elevation grasslands and foothills, primarily south and east of the area covered in this book. The California Tiger typically breeds in ephemeral ponds. Transformed individuals are often associated with ground squirrel and pocket gopher burrows. The California Tiger Salamander has experienced rapid population declines in recent years due primarily to loss of breeding habitat.

IDAHO GIANT SALAMANDER

Dicamptodon aterrimus   COPE

Author: Albert G. Wilson, Jr.

Description: The adult Idaho Giant Salamander is the only **dark, heavy-bodied** salamander within its geographic range. Mature individuals can measure more than 135 mm SVL and 228 mm TL. The **tail is relatively short and laterally compressed.** The feet lack tubercles, and toes are short and thick. Metamorphosed individuals are **dark brown or slate colored, usually with gray to light brown marbling on dorsal surfaces.** The venter is free of marbling and somewhat pale compared to the dorsum. Paedomorphic adults typically have a **purple-brown dorsum without light marbling,** and a bluish gray venter. Paedomorphs can be as short as 107 mm SVL. Larval Idaho Giant Salamanders are stream adapted with **short, bushy, red gills**

and a short dorsal fin. Typically, young larvae are brown dorsally, without marbling, and have a whitish venter. They have pale stripes behind the eyes and a darkened tail tip that lightens with age. Older larvae resemble paedomorphs.

Variation: In terrestrial forms, there are two distinct patterns of dorsal marbling seen within populations. In one, individuals have marbling over the entire dorsum. Less commonly, the mid-dorsum is plain, and marbling is restricted to the sides. There is also some subtle geographic variation in marbling density, with the finest grain pattern occurring in individuals from the southern part of the species' range.

Eggs and Larvae: Eggs are white and attached singly to rocks and possibly other substrates by short pedicels. Eggs average 6.1 mm in diameter. A female can lay as many as 185 eggs in a nest site. The size of hatchlings has not been reported in Idaho Giant Salamanders, but larvae measuring 50 mm TL have been reported. Larvae may metamorphose at 140–180 mm SVL.

Similar Species: Terrestrial Tiger Salamanders have yellow, green or olive blotching against a black ground color. Tiger Salamanders also have tubercles on the hind feet and longer tails relative to body length than do Idaho Giant Salamanders. Larvae of Tiger Salamanders and Long-toed Salamanders are pond adapted, with long dorsal fins and long gills. The Idaho Giant is most similar to the Coastal Giant Salamander but is darker and has finer marbling.

Distribution: This is the sole *Dicamptodon* of the Rocky Mountains. Much terrain potentially inhabited by the Idaho Giant Salamander has not been surveyed, and distribution of this species is poorly documented. Most known localities are in western drainages of the Bitterroot Range of Idaho. A possibly disjunct set of populations also resides farther south in the

Transformed adult

*Benewah County,
Idaho*

Transformed adult

*Benewah County,
Idaho*

**Transformed adult
(under water)**

*Benewah County,
Idaho*

Transformed adult in defensive posture
Valley County, Idaho

Portrait of a transformed adult
Benewah County, Idaho

Larva
Benewah County, Idaho

Salmon River drainage. Records indicate the Idaho Giant Salamander also may occur on the east slope of the Bitterroots in Montana. Elevational limits for the species have not been reported, but Idaho Giants can be regionally common in streams above 975 m.

Life History: Idaho Giant Salamanders probably breed during spring and fall in headwater streams, although courtship has not been observed in this species. The incubation period is unknown. Idaho Giant Salamanders are slow to mature, possibly due to a relatively short growing season in the Rockies. Individuals in the Palouse drainage of northern Idaho metamorphose in their third year.

Natural History: Populations of Idaho Giant Salamanders may include both terrestrial and paedomorphic forms. Larvae eat aquatic invertebrates and Rocky Mountain Tailed Frog tadpoles. The diet of terrestrial Idaho Giant Salamanders has not been reported, but they likely are opportunistic predators, taking invertebrates and small vertebrates. Predators of Idaho Giant Salamanders probably include trout, gartersnakes, Mink, River Otters and birds. Terrestrial adults exhibit a defensive posture in which the back is arched and tail is used to whip attackers with presumably noxious skin secretions.

Habitat: Idaho Giant Salamanders inhabit moist coniferous forests, typically in steep terrain. Larvae and paedomorphs can be found in cold, fast-moving streams and sometimes mountain lakes or ponds. Terrestrial forms take shelter during the day under rocks or woody debris in or near water. Although they can be active during the day in damp weather, they are most readily seen at night. A good way to observe terrestrial Idaho Giant Salamanders is to drive streamside forest roads and search by headlight on warm, rainy nights.

Remarks: The Idaho Giant Salamander is the most poorly studied member of its genus. Little is known of its habits and natural history. In the 1980s, genetic analyses distinguished *Dicamptodon aterrimus* from other species of Pacific giant salamanders. Older literature refers to the Idaho Giant Salamander as *Dicamptodon ensatus.*

COPE'S GIANT SALAMANDER

Dicamptodon copei   NUSSBAUM

Authors: Lawrence L.C. Jones and R. Bruce Bury

Description: This species is usually found in its larval or paedomorphic state. It is the smallest of the genus, reaching only about 200 mm TL and 120 mm SVL, whether it is a paedomorphic or terrestrial adult. Although rarely found, transformed terrestrial adults usually possess a small head, short limbs and **relatively large eyes that are close together.** The **ground color of this species is dark brown, which is most apparent on the venter.** There are a **plain color and a marbled phase.** Paedomorphic adults have a small, somewhat **rectangular or slightly hourglass-shaped head** (viewed from above), and **short legs.** The toe tips usually **do not touch when adpressed.** Paedomorphs are **dark brown with distinct**

yellowish tan patches; the skin is usually **granular in appearance.** The **venter is slate gray in color.** Paedomorphs can be distinguished from larvae by the more granular skin and protruding eyes.

Variation: The **plain phase terrestrial form has the dark ground color of the species but lacks marbling or has marbling limited to the head and/or forelimbs and forebody.** This form has been found only in the Cascade Range of Washington, but it may occur elsewhere. The more common (but still rare) form is the **marbled phase, which has fine marbling and bold, coppery reticulations on the body that are narrower than the dark reticulations.** This marbled form typically has a **light band on the outer margin of the eyelid.** In some populations, paedomorphs are dark overall and lack light patches, or the patches are few and may be aggregated near the head. A partial albino larva has been reported from the Washington Cascade Range.

Eggs and Larvae: Few nests and eggs are known for Cope's Giant Salamander. The known clutches have been found under large objects in streams. Females usually deposit about 50 eggs (but may deposit three times as many), suspended from rocks and logs in the stream. Eggs are white to cream colored, encased in about a 5.5 mm gelatinous coat. Larvae hatch at about 20 mm TL and live off their yolk until they are about 35 mm. Larvae have large **white to yellowish tan blotches** on a darker background dorsally, with a whitish to cream venter. They lack granular skin glands and protruding eyes. Larvae usually become paedomorphic adults at about 65–75 mm SVL.

Similar Species: The Coastal Giant Salamander is the only other member of the genus that is sympatric with Cope's. Small larvae of these species are sometimes difficult to distinguish because they are similar in proportions, but Coastal Giant

Transformed adult
*Lewis County,
Washington*

Transformed adult
*Lewis County,
Washington*

Transformed adult
*Grays Harbor County,
Washington*

**Portrait of a
transformed adult**
*Pacific County,
Washington*

WILLIAM LEONARD

Paedomorph
*Grays Harbor County,
Washington*

WILLIAM LEONARD

**Portrait of
a larva**
*Skamania County,
Washington*

WILLIAM LEONARD

Salamanders usually have a lighter dorsum and lack distinct, large, yellowish tan patches against a darker background. As larvae grow, Coastal Giants usually retain a light venter, while Cope's develop a dark venter. Larger Coastal Giant larvae and adults are a more robust species and have a larger head and longer limbs than Cope's Giants do. When the limbs of the Coastal Giant Salamander are adpressed, they usually overlap. Cope's paedomorphs and large larvae have less bushy gills than Coastal Giants. Coastal Giants can reach a larger maximum size and have a mass that is more than six times that of Cope's. Transformed Coastal Giants never have a "plain phase," but large individuals have a subdued pattern due to fading that develops with senescence. Terrestrial Coastal Giants have a more coarsely marbled pattern than Cope's, with the lighter reticulations narrower than the dark reticulations.

Distribution: The range of this species is not completely known. It is found on the Olympic Peninsula but appears to be rare to absent from the northeastern portion. In southwestern Washington, it is widespread in Pacific County (including Long Island) and western Lewis County, and it is known from parts of Wahkiakum County. In the Washington Cascade Range, it occurs from tributaries of the Columbia River to just south of Mount Rainier National Park. In Oregon, it is known from the northern portion of the state from Clatsop County on the Pacific coast eastward to Wasco County.

Life History: Cope's Giants reputedly mate from spring through fall, but courtship and time of oviposition have not been reported. Females guard the nest from intruders, including other *Dicamptodon*. Cope's Giant Salamanders are usually considered a near-obligate paedomorphic species, but there are numerous recent records of metamorphosed animals from southwestern Washington.

Natural History: Cope's Giants often share their stream habitats with Coastal Giant Salamanders (except in the Olympic Peninsula), as well as Olympic Tailed Frogs, torrent salamanders (except Southern Torrent Salamander) and Cutthroat Trout. Predators include gartersnakes and Coastal Giant Salamanders. Cope's Giants feed on aquatic invertebrates, eggs of their own species, and tailed frogs, and they appear to be active primarily at night.

Habitat: Cope's Giant Salamanders usually occur in small, rocky streams of coniferous or mixed forests and are especially abundant in pools in the streams, often under large rocks. Sometimes Cope's Giants also occur in mountain lakes. They are most abundant in undisturbed forests but are somewhat resilient to logging and usually recover as the forest matures. Small larvae are often seen in the edges of streams.

Remarks: There has been little research on this species since it was described in 1970. Before that time, Cope's was thought to be a variant of the Coastal Giant Salamander. We now have a better grasp on the distributional limits of this species. We know that metamorphosis in some populations is not as rare as previously believed, and the degree of sympatry with Coastal Giants is high in some areas. However, much remains to be learned about this species.

CALIFORNIA GIANT SALAMANDER

Dicamptodon ensatus   ESCHSCHOLTZ

Authors: Gary M. Fellers and Shawn R. Kuchta

Description: The California Giant Salamander is a **large, heavy-bodied** salamander with somewhat longer legs and tail than other species of *Dicamptodon.* The **backs and sides of subadults and adults have a beautiful marbled pattern** of tan, gray-brown or reddish brown, overlaid with dark brown, mocha, copper or silver blotches. The underside is whitish. Marbling or blotching on the lower jaw often extends onto the chin, throat and underside of the forelimbs and pectoral girdle. Size ranges from 115 mm SVL at metamorphosis to around 170 mm SVL. Total length may be up to 304 mm. Larvae are plain light brown dorsally with white on the venter. Older larvae are sometimes yellowish white ventrally. A light yellow stripe extends

from the back of the eye downward toward the shoulder. The short, somewhat inconspicuous gills are dark purple. While larvae occasionally have some dark mottling on the tail fin, there is rarely any dorsal pattern, especially on individuals from near San Francisco Bay and to the south.

Variation: Marbling on subadults and younger adults is often sharply defined. Older adults often lose the bright, distinct marbling, with some individuals becoming a rather plain brown except on the head, where some patterning is retained. Adults from south of San Francisco Bay have more extensive mottling on the chin than do animals to the north. Some individuals of underground cave systems are more lightly colored than stream-dwelling paedomorphs.

Eggs and Larvae: Little information is available on the location of nests or the number of eggs. Like the nests of other species of *Dicamptodon,* the few nests of *D. ensatus* that have been found have been in running water and are located well underground. The number of eggs ranges from 70–100. Each egg is about 5.5–8.5 mm in diameter and is attached to a rock or log via a stalk. Eggs are guarded by the female until they hatch, which takes several months. The larvae have a stream-type morphology, with a low tail fin extending only to the hind limbs. Larvae transform into the adult stage in their second or third year.

Similar Species: Adult and larval California Giant Salamanders have larger heads than their northern relatives, but this is difficult to judge subjectively. Adult Coastal Giant Salamanders do not have marbling that extends beyond the lower jaw onto the chin or throat. Southern Torrent Salamander *(Rhyacotriton variegatus)* larvae are superficially similar to small California Giant Salamander larvae, but torrent sal-amanders have yellow venters. In addition, the ranges of these two species do not

Transformed adult
*Santa Cruz County,
California*

WILLIAM LEONARD

Transformed adult
*Santa Cruz County,
California*

WILLIAM LEONARD

Transformed adult
*Santa Cruz County,
California*

WILLIAM LEONARD

Transformed adult
*Santa Cruz County,
California*

Transformed adult
*Sonoma County,
California*

Larva
*Marin County,
California*

overlap. California Tiger Salamanders (*Ambystoma californiense*) have large yellow or white spots and inhabit different habitats (with very limited overlap to the range of this field guide).

Distribution: The California Giant Salamander is restricted to central coastal California and has two separate distributions. In the north, it is distributed from near Point Arena in southern Mendocino County south to Marin County and east to Lake County. In the south, it is found in San Mateo and Santa Cruz Counties. The California Giant Salamander is not found east of San Francisco Bay, nor is it found in San Francisco or northern San Mateo Counties. An isolated population may exist along the coast in central Monterey County, but this has not been confirmed. The California Giant Salamander distribution overlaps that of the Coastal Giant Salamander in southern Mendocino County less than 5 km north of Anchor Bay, where hybrids of these two forms have been found. Inland from the coastal streams in Mendocino County, the distributional limits of the California and Coastal Giant Salamanders have not been documented.

Life History: Data on the life history of the California Giant Salamander are limited. Adults probably mate from spring through fall, and eggs are laid in the fall and spring. Females have been found guarding nests in March and June. Since females guard the nest until the eggs hatch, it is unlikely that they breed annually. Metamorphosis from the larval stage to the adult stage occurs from the spring through the fall at age 2 years for most individuals, and less commonly at age 3.

Natural History: Paedomorphosis occurs in some parts of the range, but it is less common in *D. ensatus* than in the other species of *Dicamptodon*. In the southern portion of the range, paedomorphic

populations are known to inhabit underground cave systems. Almost no information is available on the food habits of larval or adult California Giant Salamanders, but their diet is likely similar to that of other species of *Dicamptodon*. Both larvae and adults probably feed mostly on invertebrates and occasionally on small vertebrates such as fish, mice, snakes and other salamanders. There is one record of an adult feeding on a smaller conspecific. Adult California Giant Salamanders have a bark-like vocalization. Vocalizations have not been recorded in *Dicamptodon* outside of California and may be restricted to *D. ensatus*.

Habitat: Adults are usually found in the vicinity of permanent or semi-permanent streams in dark, wet, coniferous forests. Though adults are occasionally encountered wandering in the woods (or even going across roads) during fall rains, they are more commonly seen at night peering out of burrows along stream banks or road cuts. Adults are most easily found by looking for their eyeshine. When spotted, California Giants often back out of sight. Larvae are confined to the cool, shaded waters of streams. They are more readily observed than adults and can be seen year-round. They can often be found in the residual pools of an otherwise dry creek.

Remarks: The sharp boundary between *D. ensatus* and *D. tenebrosus* over a distance of only 2.5 km indicates that *Dicamptodon* are sedentary (at least in that part of the range) and do not travel far from their natal stream. It also suggests there is strong natural selection against hybrids. In many areas where roads follow streams, road kill mortality of adults on rainy nights is a problem. Be aware of salamanders on rainy nights, and if one is found, move it off the road in the direction of the stream.

COASTAL GIANT SALAMANDER

Dicamptodon tenebrosus   BAIRD AND GIRARD

Author: Hartwell H. Welsh, Jr.

Description: Formerly the Pacific Giant Salamander, **this is the largest salamander in the Pacific Northwest.** These robust salamanders have a large head and body with large, muscular legs. Terrestrial adults reach 190 mm SVL and 330 mm TL. **Adults have a marbled dorsum,** tan to gold on a reddish brown, chocolate or slate gray background. Undersides are gray to tan and lack patterning. Parotoid glands are not present, costal grooves are inconspicuous, and **limbs touch or overlap when adpressed against the body.** Paedomorphs are generally drab slate gray, tan or brown, with little or no patterning. Paedomorphs have short, bushy gills and shovel-shaped heads. The dorsal tail fin extends forward to the hind limbs. Paedomorphs can reach 355 mm TL.

Variation: Occasional individuals have sparse marbling or lack markings altogether. Larvae and paedomorphs vary from having no pattern to being highly mottled.

Eggs and Larvae: Eggs, deposited in clusters, are attached to undersurfaces of large rocks, logs or timbers embedded in stream channels or banks, where underground chambers with flowing water have formed. Larval morphology is similar to that of paedomorphs. Metamorphosis occurs between 92 and 166 mm TL, with sexual maturity reached at 115 mm SVL or larger.

Similar Species: Coastal Giants are sympatric with Cope's Giant Salamanders across the range of the latter, except for the Olympic Peninsula, and may occupy the same stream. Cope's Giant Salamander has a narrower head, and the adpressed limbs seldom touch or overlap; larvae and paedomorphs also have yellow or tan glandular patches present on the back and sides. The two species are not known to hybridize. At the southern end of their range, Coastal Giants are sympatric with California Giant Salamanders. In a few streams of southern Mendocino County in California, Coastal Giants are known to hybridize with the California Giant Salamander. Both larvae and adults of these two species are similar in physical appearance and thus not readily distinguishable. Larvae of the Northwestern Salamander have longer gills and longer dorsal tail fins, and they lack mottling.

Distribution: Coastal Giants are known from Mendocino County, California, north to southwestern British Columbia, through the Coast and Cascade Ranges exclusive of the Olympic Peninsula, from sea level to 2160 m. They occur widely throughout most of their range.

Life History: Courtship and mating have not been described. Terrestrial females migrate from upland habitats to streams to oviposit. Eggs have been found from spring into fall, suggesting little synchrony in

Transformed adult
*Multnomah County,
Oregon*

WILLIAM LEONARD

Transformed adult
*King County,
Washington*

KLAUS O. RICHTER

Larva
*Multnomah County,
Oregon*

WILLIAM LEONARD

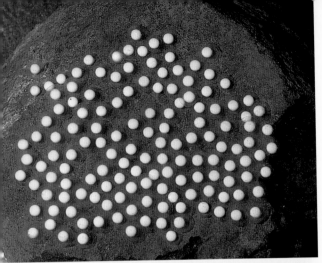

Eggs
*Benton County,
Oregon*

Larva
*Humboldt County,
California*

Larva
*Thurston County,
Washington*

breeding activity. Females lay clusters of 135–200 unpigmented eggs, individually attached by pedicels to the undersides of large rocks or logs. Females tend nests until eggs hatch and larvae disperse. Larvae metamorphose 18–24 or more months after hatching. Nothing is known about longevity, but other large, aquatic salamanders can live up to 25 years or more.

Natural History: This species exhibits facultative paedomorphosis; paedomorphic populations typically occupy perennial habitats, while small streams that may dry up harbor metamorphic or mixed populations. Larvae and paedomorphs can reach high densities, comprising a relatively high total biomass, becoming the dominant predator in many regional streams. Coastal Giants can be the most abundant stream vertebrate throughout their range. New metamorphs move out of streams to the surrounding habitat during rainy and wet periods. According to a telemetry study of terrestrial individuals in British Columbia, most movement was nocturnal or during wet periods, and individuals rarely moved beyond natal drainages, suggesting poor dispersal capabilities. Aquatic forms appear even more sedentary and may occupy the same pool or riffle for years, where they retreat under the same favored boulders or logs. They remain active in aquatic habitats during spring, summer and fall, moving mostly at night.

Predators include Raccoons, otters, water shrews, gartersnakes, salmonid fishes and conspecifics. Anti-predator defenses include biting, arching, tail-lashing and exudation of noxious skin secretions. Larvae are known to feed on aquatic invertebrates, including insect larvae and adults, mollusks and crayfish, as well as some vertebrates, including other *Dicamptodon*, other amphibians and salmonids. Adult Coastal Giant Salamanders are sit-and-wait predators that can lunge short distances with surprising speed to procure invertebrates (banana slugs are a favorite) and vertebrates, including small birds, reptiles and mammals.

Habitat: Terrestrial Coastal Giant Salamanders occur in moist forests. They seek refuge under rocks and logs, and in root channels and mammal burrows. Habitat use patterns from a telemetry study of terrestrial animals demonstrated that they may select near-stream habitats in more developed forest (e.g., old forests or younger forest stands with wide stream buffers). Larvae and paedomorphs are found primarily in lotic waters, from headwaters to rivers, but can also occur in lentic habitats such as mountain lakes. While some research has found aquatic giant salamanders more abundant in streams in late-seral forests compared with harvested or younger forests, other studies have reported no such effect, or a contrary relationship. Most studies have noted that within-stream conditions were better predictors of presence and abundance than were surrounding forest conditions. Along partially shaded and adequately buffered streams, within-stream habitat diversity appears to support the highest abundances and the full range of size classes of aquatic Coastal Giant Salamanders. This within-stream diversity includes both a range of coarse substrate sizes (from boulders to pebbles with little fine sediment) and a good mix of pools, riffles and runs.

Remarks: Several studies on sedimentation found Coastal Giant Salamanders at higher densities in streams with few fine sediments. Increased siltation negatively affects cover by filling interstices between and under coarse substrates. Despite the negative effects of such habitat alterations on Coastal Giants, they seem to be more resilient than other co-occurring, stream-associated amphibians and are likely to persist under moderate disturbance.

CASCADE TORRENT SALAMANDER

Rhyacotriton cascadae   GOOD AND WAKE

Author: Charles M. Crisafulli

Description: The Cascade Torrent Salamander is small, measuring to about 56 mm SVL and 105 mm TL. Females are larger than males by 2–4 mm, and **males possess prominent vent glands that are posteriorly squared-off** and extend out beyond the body trunk. Cascade Torrent Salamanders have a short snout and large, bulging eyes that extend well above and beyond the outline of the head. The tail is short and laterally compressed. Cascade Torrent Salamanders have 14–15 faint costal grooves. The dorsum is brown, tan or olive with spots or blotches of black and small flecks of white. The lateral surfaces are yellowish, with abundant white flecking and some black spots, typically along the dorsal edge. The **venter is**

usually bright yellow, with few black spots and small white flecking.

Variation: Among populations, Cascade Torrent Salamanders exhibit substantial variation in the amount and pattern of pigmentation. For example, in areas around Mount St. Helens, animals often occur that have "salt and pepper" dorsal and lateral surfaces, and the ventral surface often has numerous, large black spots against a very bright yellow ground color. In contrast, animals from the East Fork Lewis River have dorsal surfaces with few, small black spots, and white flecking is largely absent. The lateral surfaces have moderate levels of white flecking, and the ventral surface is light yellow, with few or no black spots, and little white pigmentation. These geographic areas are 40–50 km apart.

Eggs and Larvae: Nests of this species have never been found. However, they are likely similar to those described for the Columbia Torrent Salamander. The average clutch size from collected animals is 8 (range 2–13). Hatchlings emerge at about 16 mm SVL. Larvae have stream-dwelling morphology with **diminutive gills that are barely visible,** streamlined body shape and a greatly reduced tail fin that does not extend forward beyond the vent. The dorsum is light brown or tan, variably speckled with black. The sides and venter are cream to light yellow, with varying amounts of black spotting. Larvae metamorphose at about 40 mm SVL.

Similar Species: The three other torrent salamanders found in the Pacific Northwest do not have ranges that overlap with that of the Cascade Torrent Salamander. In Washington, the light phase of the Van Dyke's Salamander has nasolabial grooves, distinct costal grooves and no black spotting. In Oregon, the Dunn's Salamander has a greenish or gold dorsal stripe, distinct costal grooves, no black spotting on the dorsum and a lateral surface

Adult
*Multnomah County,
Oregon*

WILLIAM LEONARD

Adult
*Skamania County,
Washington*

WILLIAM LEONARD

Adult
*Skamania County,
Washington*

WILLIAM LEONARD

Adult
Multnomah County, Oregon

Underside of an adult female
Multnomah County, Oregon

Larva
Skamania County, Washington

with large flecks of dorsal stripe color. In addition, Dunn's Salamander is considerably larger than the Cascade Torrent Salamander. The larvae of Pacific giant salamanders have longer snouts, larger gills, larger and more robust bodies and a lack of black spots dorsally.

Distribution: The Cascade Torrent Salamander is endemic to the west slope of the Cascade Range in Washington and Oregon. Its range extends north to about the Cowlitz River and State Route 12 in Washington, and south to the Middle Fork of the Willamette River in Oregon. Within this area, the animal is patchily distributed. In Washington, there is a single disjunct site north of the main geographic range located on the Skookumchuck River, Thurston County. Cascade Torrent Salamanders have been found from 50–1350 m in elevation.

Life History: Courtship has not been described. The species has a prolonged breeding season, lasting perhaps 8 months in some parts of its range, with peak egg-laying in spring or early summer. If similar to other *Rhyacotriton* species, Cascade Torrent Salamanders have an embryonic period of about 1 year (including incubation and post-hatching, pre-feeding stages). Larval development lasts for about 4–5 years. The average larval growth rate is about 0.3–0.7 mm per month. There appears to be a delayed maturity—the stages from embryo through maturation are a protracted process taking 5.5–6.0 years. Longevity of wild animals is unknown.

Natural History: Cascade Torrent Salamanders are surface-active throughout the spring, summer and autumn at high elevations and year-round in areas lacking deep snow pack. This species is largely nocturnal, but during heavy rains, it may be surface-active during the day. The diet of the Cascade Torrent Salamander is undocumented and likely varies by location, season and life history stage. Larval salamanders likely take aquatic invertebrates. Metamorphosed salamanders probably prey on aquatic and terrestrial invertebrates. In turn, Cascade Torrent Salamanders are likely preyed upon by Pacific giant salamanders (*Dicamptodon* species), gartersnakes, water shrews and large, predatory insects. Cascade Torrent Salamanders are known to occur with Van Dyke's, Cope's Giant, Coastal Giant, Western Red-backed and Dunn's Salamanders, and Olympic Tailed Frogs.

Habitat: Cascade Torrent Salamanders require cool, wet environments. Both larvae and metamorphosed individuals occur in microhabitats along high-gradient, cold, rock-dominated stream courses and near seeps. The aquatic larvae are associated with valley and head-wall seeps and spray zones at the base of waterfalls and cascades, where gravels and cobbles are present with shallow (< 1 cm), low-velocity flows. Metamorphosed individuals are often interspersed among the larvae or on stream banks beneath rock or wood. Transformed animals are usually within 1 m of water, but during prolonged precipitation events, they occasionally may be found > 10 m from water.

Remarks: Cascade Torrent Salamanders survived in numerous locations in areas severely impacted by the 1980 eruption of Mount St. Helens. These populations have persisted in areas of complete vegetation removal, suggesting that forest cover may not be a critical habitat feature at higher elevations.

COLUMBIA TORRENT SALAMANDER

Rhyacotriton kezeri   GOOD AND WAKE

Authors: Marc P. Hayes and Kevin R. Russell

Description: The Columbia Torrent Salamander is small (66 mm SVL) and bicolored, with **beige-brown dorsal surfaces and lemon yellow ventral surfaces.** It has large, dark, protruding eyes, moderate-sized limbs with unwebbed yellow feet, and a tail about 50% of its body length. On dorsal surfaces, white flecks are concentrated on the lower sides; black flecking is rare. **Adult males have a distinctive, square vent.** Females grow larger than males.

Eggs and Larvae: Eggs, known from few descriptions, are round, cream or white, and relatively large (4–6 mm in diameter). They are set in a near-transparent, multi-layered jelly capsule and may be coated with sediments. Close observation has revealed pits in the outer capsular layer of some eggs. The eggs are laid without attachments to other eggs or surfaces. Egg size is similar to that of some plethodontid salamanders, but capsules of the latter are rough to the touch and attached to either other eggs or surfaces. Larvae look like transformed animals except for their smaller size, less contrasting coloration between dorsal and ventral surfaces, less protruding eyes, and presence of gills and tail fins. Similar to the larval gills of other torrent salamander species, the Columbia Torrent's gills are tiny and almost impossible to see when the animal is out of water. The smallest larvae recorded (9 mm SVL) are smaller than those recorded for other torrent salamander species and may approximate size at hatching. The largest larvae recorded are 36 mm SVL, but size at metamorphosis may vary geographically or with environmental conditions.

Similar Species: The four species of torrent salamanders are generally hard to tell apart. Geography provides the best clue to identification. The Cascade Torrent Salamander, the easiest species to identify, has bold, black dorsal spots. Ensatinas and Rough-skinned Newts are also bicolored, but dorsal surfaces are darker brown, and ventral surfaces are different shades of orange. Rough-skinned Newts also have thicker, granular skin, reach a larger size and have smaller, paler eyes. Ensatinas have a constriction near the tail base, orange marks on upper limbs, and gray feet. Columbia Torrent Salamander larvae are difficult to distinguish from those of other torrent salamander species, but they can be told from the larvae of other salamanders in the Northwest by their yellow undersurfaces, extremely reduced gills and generally smaller size. The eggs cannot be distinguished from those of the Southern Torrent Salamander, the only other torrent salamander for which an egg description exists.

Distribution: Columbia Torrent Salamanders have a Coast Range distribution from the Little Nestucca River,

Adult female
Pacific County,
Washington

Adult male
Pacific County,
Washington

Adult male
Pacific County,
Washington

Adult male
*Pacific County,
Washington*

WILLIAM LEONARD

**Underside of
gravid female**
*Lewis County,
Washington*

WILLIAM LEONARD

Larva
*Pacific County,
Washington*

WILLIAM LEONARD

Oregon, to the Chehalis River, Washington. The farthest known points inland are near Ryderwood, Washington, and St. Helens, Oregon. Columbia Torrents are found from near sea level to the highest points in coastal northwestern Oregon (Saddleback Mountain, 1001 m) and southwestern Washington (Boisfort Peak, 948 m). Over this range, they are broadly distributed but seem more common in headwater habitats.

Life History: Timing of egg-laying is thought to peak in spring or early summer. Only five Columbia Torrent Salamander oviposition sites have been described. These sites had 7–75 individual, unattached eggs. Three sites likely involved eggs from more than one female (presumed average clutch size was 8–10). All sites were concealed in low-flow headwater habitats. Whether parental care exists remains unclear. Time required for development to hatching, metamorphosis and sexual maturity is unknown, but based on data for other torrent salamanders, development to sexual maturity may require more than 5 years. Longevity is also unknown.

Natural History: In headwater habitats, where Columbia Torrent Salamanders are common, co-occurrence with other species is relatively infrequent. Rare co-occurrence with Coastal Giant Salamanders was attributed to potential predation by Pacific giant salamanders. However, recent work has revealed that Southern Torrent Salamander larvae seem distasteful to giant salamanders, and shrews also reject them. The seemingly lower stream flow requirements of torrent salamanders and higher flow needs of Pacific giant salamanders might better explain their infrequent co-occurrence. Diet is unstudied, but that of adults is expected to be similar to that described for the Southern Torrent Salamander. Anecdotal data suggest that Columbia Torrents make seasonal movements away from seeps, springs and streams when adjacent upland habitats are moist, and they re-concentrate around these habitats as uplands dry.

Habitat: Columbia Torrent Salamanders occur over a broad range of low-flow aquatic habitats, including seeps, springs of smaller-order streams, and backwater and off-channel habitats of larger streams. The relationship to low-flow habitats may be linked to the unique torrent salamander oviposition pattern, in which eggs are not attached to a substrate. The few reproductive habitats described, all from springs and first-order streams, were within the cracked recesses of sandstone, under cobble and gravel or beneath moss mats. The rarity with which egg sites have been found in contrast to the species' high abundance implies that Columbia Torrent Salamanders often deposit eggs in inaccessible places. Recent work in Washington and Oregon suggests that Columbia Torrents are more common in steeper streams with more cobble and gravel. They also may be more abundant on slower-weathering basalt (volcanic) geologies than on faster-weathering sedimentary geologies (mudstones and siltstones). This relationship may arise from slower-weathering geologies having more cobble and gravel and fewer fine sediments than faster-weathering ones.

Remarks: Columbia Torrent Salamanders are among the most observable and likely most abundant amphibians across most of their geographic range. As over 95% of their range has been managed extensively for timber production, the high densities (up to 70 salamanders/m^2) of Columbia Torrent Salamanders observed seem to contradict the often-quoted dogma that forestry practices eliminate torrent salamanders. This apparent contradiction remains unexplained, but it may reflect the fact that the species' range falls almost entirely within a relatively high rainfall coastal region.

OLYMPIC TORRENT SALAMANDER

Rhyacotriton olympicus   GAIGE

Authors: R. Bruce Bury and Lawrence L.C. Jones

Description: This is a small salamander, measuring 50–55 mm SVL and 90–97 mm TL. The body is stout; legs and tail are short. The head has large, protruding eyes. The dorsum is brown or olive, with a scattering of white spots on the sides. The **venter is yellow, yellowish green or yellowish orange, with few dark specks. The demarcation line between dorsal and ventral colors is wavy.** The **male has external, squarish vent lobes,** a trait unique to this group of salamanders.

Eggs and Larvae: No eggs or nests for this species have been found, but Olympic Torrent Salamanders are expected to have few eggs because ovarian egg counts from collected females averaged 8 eggs. Like their close relative, the Columbia Torrent

Salamander, Olympic Torrents may nest in seeps with coarse substrates. Eggs are likely deposited singly, surrounded by 6 jelly layers, and are likely white and large at 3.0–4.5 mm in diameter. The larvae appear as miniatures of the adults but have short gills (an adaptation for brook life), and the dorsal color is more yellow. Larvae are tan to brown above, and black dots occur over the entire body. The venter is whitish to yellowish and appears almost translucent through the belly wall. The eyes do not protrude, as they do in adults.

Similar Species: Olympic Torrent Salamanders are distinct from all other salamanders on the Olympic Peninsula because of their bright yellow venter, although Rough-skinned Newts have an orange venter. Other torrent salamander species may be differentiated by dorsal and ventral spotting and the form of the demarcation line, but these subtle differences are moot in the field: Olympic Torrents do not coexist with any other species of torrent salamander. The tiny gills and overall pale color differentiate the larvae of Olympic Torrent Salamanders from Pacific giant salamanders, which have a dark brown dorsum, white to gray venter and bushier gills.

Distribution: This species occurs only on the Olympic Peninsula in northwestern Washington, extending south to near the Chehalis River. Olympic Torrent Salamanders range up to about 1200 m elevation in the Olympic Mountains, but most occur below 1000 m.

Life History: Courting and breeding have not been observed in this species, but the breeding season may extend over most of the year. Few nests or eggs have been found in the wild for any species of torrent salamanders. Females of other species of *Rhyacotriton* appear to nest communally, as eggs (32 and 72 in two nests) exceeded egg counts in individual females collected for

Adult male

Jefferson County, Washington

Adult male

Mason County, Washington

Portrait of larva showing minute gills
Jefferson County, Washington

Larva
Jefferson County, Washington

Larva
Jefferson County, Washington

study (most have 6–12 eggs). Clutch size increases with body size. Eggs held at a temperature of 8°C hatched after 210–290 days in the laboratory. Larvae grow slowly and transform at about 40–45 mm SVL when 3–4 years old.

Natural History: As with the other torrent salamander species, Olympic Torrent Salamanders are sensitive to loss of body water and will die quickly in dry environments. Thus, they are closely tied to wet areas. They select cool waters (12–14°C) in laboratory experiments. Olympic Torrent Salamanders likely feed on a variety of invertebrates. Their predators include Pacific giant salamanders, which eat their eggs but may avoid eating larvae or adults. Gartersnakes are likely predators. Torrent salamanders have noxious skin secretions that repel attacks from shrews and perhaps other small mammals. Olympic Torrent Salamanders often occur with Olympic Tailed Frogs, Cope's Giant Salamanders, Van Dyke's Salamanders and Western Red-backed Salamanders in seep and stream habitats. Olympic Torrent Salamanders may reach high densities in good habitat, and they may be active day or night, depending on ambient temperature and moisture conditions.

Habitat: Most populations are in cool, temperate, coastal areas or on north-facing slopes in the interior of the Olympic Peninsula. They frequent flowing-water habitats on steep slopes. Olympic Torrent Salamanders are associated with cool or cold-water seeps, waterfalls, headwaters and edges of larger streams. Individuals occur under rocks in the splash zone or on moss-covered rocks and cobble, often with their feet wet or close to water where they can dart upon exposure. During wet periods, they may move several meters away from the stream.

Remarks: Until fairly recently, all torrent salamanders were considered to belong to one species, the Olympic Salamander. Genetics studies have shown that there are four cryptic species. While they were previously placed in either family Ambystomatidae or Dicamptodontidae, they are now elevated to their own family, Rhyacotritonidae. Under certain environmental conditions, timber harvest may have a negative effect on populations of *R. olympicus*.

SOUTHERN TORRENT SALAMANDER

Rhyacotriton variegatus   STEBBINS AND LOWE

Author: Hartwell H. Welsh, Jr.

Description: The Southern Torrent Salamander has an olive or brown dorsal color, with evenly **distributed dark spotting or mottling. The belly is bright yellow, with a similar pattern of dark brown or black spots.** Fine pale or white flecks may be present over much of the head and body. Males have squared vent lobes. Adults measure 35–52 mm SVL.

Variation: Northern populations have less spotting than southern populations. The high genetic diversity among the populations suggests there may be as many as four cryptic species comprising *Rhyacotriton variegatus.*

Eggs and Larvae: Two nests with eggs were found in northern California beneath boulders in cold, clear, headwater streams

with coarse substrates; clutch sizes were 11 and 8 eggs. The larvae have short but distinct gills on the side of the head. Larger larvae are colored like adults but are less distinctly bicolored; smaller larvae are translucent gray, often with a pink hue.

Similar Species: The Columbia Torrent Salamander and Olympic Torrent both lack spotting on the dorsum. The Cascade Torrent Salamander has spots concentrated along the color demarcation between dorsum and venter.

Distribution: The Southern Torrent Salamander is locally distributed in the Coast Range of Oregon from the Little Nestucca River southward to Dark Gulch in Mendocino County, California. Populations also occur across the interior southern mountains east to the north Umpqua River drainage of the Cascade Range of southern Oregon. In California, populations are found throughout the Klamath River drainage east to near Happy Camp, with a more coastally restricted distribution southward. A disjunct population is reported to occur about 113 km east of the established range in the upper McCloud River drainage in Siskiyou County, California, but this needs further confirmation. The distribution is generally spotty, with occurrences closely linked to headwater habitats in late-seral forests.

Life History: Reproduction probably occurs in the water, but actual courtship has not been observed in the field. It is likely that breeding occurs along the shallow margins of low-order streams, springs and seeps. Egg development is slow, greater than 193–220 days. The larval period is 3.0–3.5 years. Larvae take 4.5–5.0 years to reach sexual maturity, 1–1.5 years after metamorphosis. The long maturation time suggests that this is a relatively long-lived species.

Natural History: Limited information suggests that these salamanders are highly

Adult
*Humboldt County,
California*

Adult
*Humboldt County,
California*

Adult
*Humboldt County,
California*

Underside of an adult male
Humboldt County, California

Portrait of larva showing minute gills
Humboldt County, California

Larva
Humboldt County, California

sedentary, especially as adults. No studies have addressed whether they defend territories. Both larvae and adults appear to burrow into streambed substrates in response to warm water temperatures and lower stream flows associated with summer weather conditions, and high stream flows during winter. It is not known whether larvae and adults are active in these subterranean habitats during the summer. However, greater weight gains over winter compared with summer for both life stages suggest a period of inactivity during the hotter and drier summer season, as well as some activity during the winter. Adults can move between headwater and adjacent riparian and upland habitats during wet periods. Adults eat primarily aquatic and semi-aquatic insects, most of which are larval and nymph life stages of amphipods and springtails. Coastal Giant Salamanders are known to feed on Southern Torrent Salamanders, and the selection of shallow water microhabitats on the part of the torrent salamanders may be a response to this predation.

Habitat: Southern Torrent Salamanders are usually found in headwater streams in moist, mature to late-seral forests or in proximate riparian forest habitats that provide a cool, wet microenvironment. However, in the marine-influenced coastal Redwoods of northern California and at some western Oregon sites, Southern Torrents can be found in younger seral-stage forests. Adults, while occasionally found in moist upland and riparian areas, are usually found in contact with cold (6.5–15°C), clear water in springs, seeps and headwater streams with rocky substrates. The larvae are morphologically adapted to such mountain brook microenvironments, which have low velocity flows over unsorted rock or rock rubble substrates. The high moisture requirements are probably related to the fact that species in the genus *Rhyacotriton* are the most desiccation intolerant salamanders known, a condition that may be linked to a high dependence on skin surfaces for oxygen uptake, as their lungs are greatly reduced. Several studies have documented the importance of a lack of fine sediments (fine gravel and sand) that can fill in coarse, streambed substrate interstices used for cover by both larval and adult salamanders.

Remarks: The patchy distribution of Southern Torrent Salamanders, both south and inland, likely reflects unsuitable habitat conditions, particularly the elevated stream temperatures that inland and more southern streams can attain. Elevated stream temperatures are a specific concern for this species in these portions of its range. In the south, Southern Torrent Salamanders appear particularly susceptible to habitat alterations resulting from timber harvest activities that fail to adequately protect headwaters. In this region of the range, increased stream temperatures from clear-cut harvesting practices have been particularly acute. Sedimentation also has been a concern. The distributional evidence indicates that historically this species consisted of more populations across the range than is currently the case. Consequently, the Southern Torrent Salamander has been petitioned for listing under the federal Endangered Species Act based on both loss of habitat and population declines due to forestry practices, but these efforts toward listing have so far been unsuccessful.

ROUGH-SKINNED NEWT

Taricha granulosa   SKILTON

Author: Shawn R. Kuchta

Description: Rough-skinned Newts **are brown dorsolaterally, with a bright yellow-orange to orange belly.** The eyes are **yellow above and below the iris** and are relatively small, failing to break the outline of the jaw when viewed from above. The lower eyelid is brown. Vomerine teeth form a V-shaped pattern on the roof of the mouth. The body is of medium size, averaging 59–70 mm SVL, and **lacks costal grooves.** The skin of terrestrial forms is granular and rough to the touch, like that of other newts. The appearance of males changes when they become aquatic for breeding: they develop smooth skin, dark nuptial pads, a swollen cloaca and a large tail fin. The skin color of breeding males is lighter, and their body takes on a puffy appearance. Females do not alter their overall morphology during breeding, but their cloaca takes on a cone shape. Strict paedomorphosis is unknown, but some adults at high elevations retain gills or gill stubs and do not migrate from the aquatic habitat after metamorphosis.

Variation: Older sources often recognize two subspecies, the Oregon Newt, *T. granulosa granulosa* (Skilton), and the Crater Lake Newt, *T. granulosa mazamae* (Myers). Crater Lake Newts were described as having brown dorsolateral coloration extending onto the ventral surface of the torso. Current sources usually do not recognize this subspecies, as some Crater Lake Newts lack this characteristic, while some individuals in populations outside of the Crater Lake area can look like Crater Lake Newts. It is unlikely that Crater Lake Newts constitute a distinct historical lineage separate from other Rough-skinned Newts.

Eggs and Larvae: Eggs are surrounded by a rubbery, gelatinous capsule, totaling 3–4 mm diameter, and are laid singly. Ova are tan above and cream below and can rotate in the capsule. Hatchlings are about 18 mm TL and possess a balancer organ, which is lost as the larvae grow. Rough-skinned Newts have pond-type larvae with a tall dorsal fin extending to the shoulders. The ground color is translucent tan covered with a dense stippling of small, black flecks. Larger, light spots run the length of the body on either side of the tail fin.

Similar Species: Red-bellied Newts have a tomato-red belly and a dark brown eye (no yellow). California Newts look very similar to Rough-skinned Newts, but the latter usually have a smaller eye, a V-shaped (not Y-shaped) pattern of vomerine teeth on the roof of the mouth, and a brown (not orange) lower eyelid. The Yellow-eyed Ensatina *(Ensatina eschscholtzii xanthoptica)* has smooth skin, a constriction at the base of the tail and distinct costal grooves. California and Red-bellied Newts lay their eggs in clusters, rather than singly.

Adult exhibiting a defensive posture known as the "unken" reflex
Whatcom County, Washington

Underside of an adult female
Thurston County, Washington

An egg attached to a submerged blade of grass
Thurston County, Washington

Larva
Pierce County, Washington

Juvenile
Benton County, Oregon

Distribution: Rough-skinned Newts are distributed in the coastal mountains from southeast Alaska to Santa Cruz County, California, on the north end of Monterey Bay. In northern California, they extend east through Shasta County and into northern Butte County. There are also populations near Moscow, Latah County, Idaho.

Life History: The timing of life history events is highly variable, depending on local conditions. Adults can migrate to breeding sites from December through July. At lower elevations, eggs are typically laid between January and May, with larvae metamorphosing in the late summer and fall. At high elevation sites, eggs are laid during summer and early fall, and larvae metamorphose about a year later. The eggs hatch in 3–4 weeks. Larvae usually metamorphose in the late summer or early fall after a 4–5 month larval period, at sizes from 23–75 mm TL. However, in high elevation lakes, larvae often overwinter and metamorphose in the spring or summer at sizes from 65–95 mm TL. The length of the juvenile stage is unclear, but after several years, adults return to aquatic habitats to breed and lay eggs.

Natural History: Rough-skinned Newts are conspicuous in both aquatic and terrestrial stages and are the salamander most commonly seen by many people. They are active day and night and may be seen crossing roads during spring breeding migrations. Newts often display their orange belly when threatened by potential predators by curling their head and tails over their torso, arching their back and closing their eyes. This is called an unken reflex and is a warning that the newts are poisonous. The eggs and adults of species of *Taricha* contain large amounts of a potent neurotoxin called tetrodotoxin, and this may explain the newts' diurnal nature. Fish, ducks, Bullfrogs, owls and even humans have died from eating a newt.

However, there is extensive geographic variation in levels of toxicity, with high toxicity in some areas and low toxicity in others. It is thought that extreme toxicity levels found in newts are the result of a co-evolutionary "arms race" with the Common Gartersnake, *Thamnophis sirtalis,* which can eat toxic newts. It is also thought that the Yellow-eyed Ensatina mimics Rough-skinned and California Newts and limits predation through this resemblance.

The migratory and reproductive behavior of the Rough-skinned Newt is similar to Red-bellied and California Newts. Rough-skinned Newts can make extensive overland migrations, yet they appear to have site fidelity, homing to aquatic breeding sites. Rough-skinned Newts have been shown to use celestial cues to orient to breeding sites during terrestrial movements. During breeding, a male clasps the back of a female and induces reproductive receptivity. He then dismounts and leaves a spermatophore on the pond bottom, and she picks the sperm packet off the top of the sperm-atophore with her cloaca. She subsequently oviposits fertilized eggs in the pond.

Habitat: Juvenile and adult Rough-skinned Newts are most abundant in forested habitats, including coniferous and deciduous woodlands in rolling and mountainous terrain. However, they can also occur in open valleys. Adults breed in ponds, ditches, beaver ponds and sluggish stretches of streams. Some individuals remain in aquatic habitats year-round or during the dry summer months.

Remarks: It is safe to handle newts, but wash your hands afterwards, and be wary of touching your eyes.

RED-BELLIED NEWT

Taricha rivularis   TWITTY

Author: Shawn R. Kuchta

Description: The Red-bellied Newt is a medium-sized salamander with a **dark brown to black back and a tomato-red belly.** The sides of the body **lack costal grooves,** and the **tail is keeled.** The **eyes are a solid dark brown (black to casual inspection)** and are large; when viewed from directly above, the corneal surface of the eye easily breaks the jaw outline. Teeth on the roof of the mouth **form a Y-shaped pattern.** The snout is somewhat pointed. Males have a dark band across the cloaca, but females are commonly unbanded. Adults are 50–80 mm SVL. The skin of terrestrial forms is granular, like other western newts. As with other newt species, male Red-bellied Newts have smooth skin during breeding at aquatic sites. Aquatic, breeding-condition females have a swollen

cloaca. Metamorphs are 45–55 mm TL and have the adult color pattern.

Eggs and Larvae: Eggs are laid in clusters of 5–15 (average about 9). Individual eggs are larger than in other newt species (average 2.75 mm diameter). Egg masses are rubbery, due to a firm gelatinous envelope, and are attached to the undersides of rocks and logs in areas of high water flow. Egg masses of the Red-bellied Newt are flattened, like small, thick pancakes. This seems to facilitate attachment to the underside of rocks and logs. Red-bellied Newts possess a stream-type larva, with the dorsal fin failing to reach the shoulders. The ground color of larvae is pale yellow, with black speckling distributed evenly over the sides of the body. Unlike adults' eyes, the eyes of larvae have yellow pigment surrounding the pupil. Balancer organs are rudimentary or absent.

Similar Species: All terrestrial-stage newts have a rough skin texture, unlike all other western salamanders. Red-bellied Newts are easily distinguished from other newt species by their solid brown eyes (no yellow). Relative to Rough-skinned Newts and California Newts, Red-bellied Newts have a narrow head, pointy snout and large eyes. In addition, no other salamander has a dark brown dorsum and tomato-red belly. During breeding, male Red-bellied Newts have a smaller tail fin, and the cloaca is less swollen than in other species of *Taricha.* Egg masses of California Newts are spherical, while Rough-skinned Newt eggs are oviposited singly.

Distribution: Red-bellied Newts have the most restricted distribution of any West Coast newt. They are found in the coastal region of California from near Bodega and Santa Rosa, Sonoma County, in the south, east to Lower Lake and Kelsey Creek in Lake County, and north to Honeydew, Humboldt County.

Life History: Red-bellied Newts are more highly adapted for stream breeding than the

Adult
*Humboldt County,
California*

WAYNE VAN DEVENDER

Adult
*Humboldt County,
California*

WAYNE VAN DEVENDER

**Adult exhibiting
"unken" reflex**
California

EDMUND D. BRODIE, JR.

Egg mass
*Sonoma County,
California*

Hatchling larva
*Sonoma County,
California*

Larva
*Humboldt County,
California*

California or Rough-skinned Newt. Eggs are laid during March and April in moderate- to swift-flowing, rocky streams. Eggs hatch in 2–5 weeks. Larvae feed and grow in the slower stretches of streams and can be found under rocks and logs near the water's edge. Red-bellied Newts metamorphose at the end of the summer and disperse into the surrounding forests. The juvenile stage lasts roughly 5 years, and juveniles are not often caught above ground. Small invertebrates are the primary food source. Males breed most years, but females commonly breed every second or third year. Adults can live to be 15 or more years old. Individuals tend to stay within their natal drainage; in one study, only one out of 22,000 adults was found to move voluntarily to a nearby stream.

Natural History: The reproductive behavior, ecology and migratory behavior of Red-bellied Newts were extensively studied by the late Victor Chandler Twitty, and his charming 1966 autobiography (and research summary), *Of Scientists and Salamanders,* is must-read material for all newt lovers. In one impressive demonstration of migratory ability, Red-bellied Newts that were displaced 8 km (5 mi) over two mountain ridges returned to their home stream. Moreover, they migrated overland, even though an aquatic route was possible. Adults displaced upstream or downstream within the same drainage also returned to where they were caught. Other experiments by Twitty showed that olfaction plays an important role in the homing abilities of Red-bellied Newts, but vision is not an important migratory sense. Studies on other newt species may apply to our understanding of the migratory ecology of the Red-bellied Newt. For example, the Rough-skinned Newt employs celestial cues when migrating, and the California Newt has a kinesthetic sense that detects bodily position and functions to keep individuals

moving in a consistent direction during migration. Both of these mechanisms are likely used by Red-bellied Newts as well. Finally, it was recently shown that a newt in the eastern half of the United States, the Red-spotted Newt *(Notophthalmus viridescens),* has an internal magnetic compass. Experiments have not been conducted on any species of *Taricha,* but a magnetic compass seems probable, given *Taricha's* demonstrated homing abilities.

The reproductive behavior of the Red-bellied Newt is similar to the California Newt. At breeding ponds, after a male detects a female, he approaches her and clasps her back with his forelimbs. By rubbing his chin on her snout, he applies a pheromone which serves to increase the female's receptivity to mating and helps to synchronize male and female courtship. He then dismounts and deposits a spermatophore on the pond bottom, from which she picks up a sperm packet with her cloaca. She then oviposits fertilized eggs in the water, attaching them to leaves and vegetation.

Habitat: Red-bellied Newts inhabit oak woodland and Redwood forests in the north coastal region of California. They are rarely found outside of the drainage in which they breed. Breeding occurs in cold streams with moderate to fast currents and rocky substrates.

Remarks: Like other western newts, Red-bellied Newts possess the neurotoxin known as tetrodotoxin which, if ingested, will kill most vertebrates. When harassed, the Red-bellied Newt will assume a defensive posture called the unken reflex, where the newt curls its head and tail over its torso, arching its back and closing its eyes. Natural hybridization between Red-bellied Newts and other newts is very rare, but experiments have shown that newts are physiologically capable of interbreeding in all interspecific combinations.

CALIFORNIA NEWT

Taricha torosa RATHKE

Author: Shawn R. Kuchta

Description: The California Newt is a medium-sized salamander with a **brown to orange-brown back and a pale yellow to orange belly.** The sides of the body **lack costal grooves. The tail is flattened from side to side.** The **lower eyelid color usually matches the belly color,** and the eyes are relatively large. When viewed from directly above, the corneal surface of the eye slightly breaks the jaw outline. Teeth on the roof of the mouth **form a Y-shaped pattern.** Adults are approximately 50–88 mm SVL. The skin of terrestrial forms is granular and rough. Males in breeding condition at aquatic sites undergo physical changes: the skin becomes smooth, the tail keel broadens significantly (for swimming), the soles of the feet and the undersides of the hind legs take on a dark, roughened texture like fine sand-

paper (nuptial pads, for holding onto slippery females), the toe tips become hardened, the cloaca becomes swollen and the body swells and takes on a fat, puffy appearance. Females do not change much when entering aquatic habitats to breed, but their cloacae become swollen. Metamorphs are about 45–55 mm TL and weigh half a gram. They possess the adult color pattern at metamorphosis.

Variation: The California Newt is fairly uniform throughout the range of this field guide in both genetic variation and color pattern. In the vicinity of Berkeley and Palo Alto, California, there are pond- and stream-breeding populations that appear to remain distinct even when these two habitats are in close proximity to one another. Pond breeders breed from December through February, and stream breeders breed in March and April, presumably as an adaptation for avoiding winter flooding. Two subspecies are recognized, the Coast Range Newt (*T. torosa torosa)* and the Sierra Newt (*T. torosa sierrae).* The Sierra Newt is distinctive in morphology, genetics and life history, and may be deserving of specific recognition (this is under investigation).

Eggs and Larvae: Eggs are laid in masses of 7–47 eggs, though 15–20 eggs are most common. Encased in a gelatinous envelope, masses are round and rubbery and keep their shape when lifted outside of water. Egg masses are attached to aquatic vegetation, rocks, branches and other objects, often in less than 30 cm of water. Egg masses are 15–25 mm in diameter. The upper surface of the developing egg is dark gray or olive, and the ova can rotate freely in the egg capsule. Larvae are 10–14 mm TL at hatching. Hatchling larvae have a balancer organ that is lost as the larvae grow. Larvae are pond type, with the tail fin extending to the shoulders. The ground coloration is translucent tan, with two solid

Adult

Los Angeles County, California

Adult

Los Angeles County, California

Adult
*Los Angeles County,
California*

Adult
*Los Angeles County,
California*

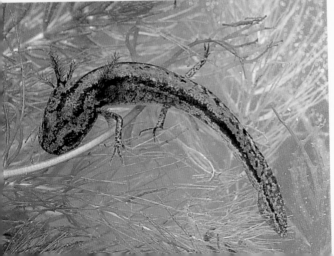

Larva
*Monterey County,
California*

lines of black flecks extending along either side of the tail fin.

Similar Species: All terrestrial newts have a rough skin texture, unlike other western salamanders. Red-bellied Newts have a tomato-red belly and no yellow in the eye. Rough-skinned Newts can be difficult to distinguish from California Newts. The latter have larger eyes, an orange lower eyelid (even though the upper lid may be brown), and vomerine teeth on the roof of the mouth forming a Y-shaped pattern (not V-shaped). The Yellow-eyed Ensatina (*Ensatina eschscholtzii xanthoptica*) has smooth skin and a constriction at the base of the tail.

Distribution: The California Newt subspecies within the range of this book is the Coast Range Newt. It is distributed coastally from central Mendocino County south to San Diego County. From Santa Cruz north into Mendocino County, the Coast Range Newt and the Rough-skinned Newt can be found in sympatry in some locations. In general, the Coast Range Newt is more abundant at inland sites, whereas the Rough-skinned Newt is more abundant nearer the coast.

Life History: Eggs are laid from December through April, depending on local conditions. The incubation time depends on water temperature and other conditions but generally requires 4–8 weeks. Larvae feed and grow for several months, and they metamorphose from late summer through early fall or when the water dries up. Metamorphs migrate from the breeding site and grow for several years prior to returning as reproductive adults, usually at > 50 mm SVL.

Natural History: Adults and juveniles are commonly active during the day. Migration between terrestrial and aquatic habitats can be extensive, up to 3200 m or more, though the typical migration distance is shorter where suitable terrestrial habitats are more readily available. During the breeding season, males move to ponds first and wait for females. When a female arrives, she is grabbed by a male, who wraps his front limbs around her torso just behind her front limbs and clings to her back. Then he rubs the underside of his chin on the top of the female's snout, thus exposing her to secretions from his submandibular gland. This increases female receptivity and synchronizes mating. After an hour or more (sometimes several hours), he dismounts and deposits a spermatophore on the pond bottom. The female squats over the spermatophore and picks up the sperm packet with her cloaca. The mating behavior of other newt species is similar. Females lay fertilized eggs, attaching them to leaves and vegetation on the edges of ponds and slow-moving stretches of creeks.

Habitat: Terrestrial adults inhabit coniferous forest and oak woodland habitats. They breed in ponds and the slower stretches of some streams.

Remarks: Newts are among the most commonly encountered salamanders, in part because of their diurnal nature. When the first fall rains arrive, California Newts become active, and reproductive adults migrate to their breeding sites. Thousands are killed annually on roads, the death toll being especially high on rainy nights. Like all western newt species, the California Newt possesses the potent neurotoxin tetrodotoxin which, if ingested, will kill most vertebrates.

CLOUDED SALAMANDER

Aneides ferreus   COPE

Author: Robert M. Storm

Description: The dorsal ground color of the Clouded Salamander is usually some shade of brown overlaid to a varying extent by brass-colored cells or patches of cells. These cells are **usually concentrated on the snout, shoulder areas and upper tail base** but may be more extensive. The underside of adults is gray. **Young animals appear to have a brassy stripe** extending from the neck to the tip of the tail, and the top of the head shows **a brass-colored triangle.** In some young, the upper tail base may appear reddish. Clouded Salamanders **have slightly expanded toe ends with squared-off tips.** The toes of adpressed limbs almost or slightly overlap. Clouded Salamanders may grow to a length of 65 mm SVL and 133 mm TL.

Variation: In general, individuals in rocky habitats seem to be more widely and brightly marked with brassy coloration than are those living in wood debris.

Eggs: During spring and early summer, eggs are deposited within cavities in large logs or stumps, or in openings deep within rocks. Each egg is fastened to the ceiling of the nest cavity by a gelatinous strand that is a continuation of the gel layer around the egg. The strands are twisted together so that they hang from one point, somewhat like a bunch of grapes. The eggs themselves are pale yellow and about 5 mm in diameter. Known clutch sizes range from 8–17 eggs. There is no free-living larval stage; hatchlings emerge as juvenile salamanders.

Similar Species: Clouded Salamanders can be distinguished from the Black Salamander by the more flattened, squared-off toe tips, gray underside and brassy wash on the back. Clouded Salamanders have an appearance similar to the Wandering Salamander, but identification usually can be inferred from geographical location, as their ranges have little overlap.

Distribution: Clouded Salamanders occur in the western Cascade Range and in the Coast Range of Oregon, from the Columbia Gorge south through the Siskiyou Mountains into northwestern California. They also occur to the South Fork Smith River headwaters in Del Norte County, California, where they overlap slightly with the range of the Wandering Salamander. They range from sea level to about 1463 m elevation. They are absent from the extreme northwestern part of the Oregon Coast Range and from the large river valleys of western Oregon.

Life History: Females are known to attend the eggs in the spring and summer, but both a male and a female occasionally may occur together at the nest. Eggs hatch in about 2 months. Limited data indicate that males may mature during

Adult
Benton County,
Oregon

Adult
Benton County,
Oregon

Portrait of an adult
Benton County,
Oregon

Juvenile
*Benton County,
Oregon*

**Adult,
adhering to glass**
*Benton County,
Oregon*

**Underside of feet
showing expanded
toe tips**
*Benton County,
Oregon*

their second year after they reach about 36 mm SVL. Females mature at a larger size after they have reached at least 55 mm SVL, and it is probable that they then produce eggs in alternate years. It is estimated that individual animals may live at least 5 years in the wild.

Natural History: Recent laboratory studies of courtship in this species showed a unique "circular tail-walk," which results in a spermatophore being transferred to the female. A study of the food habits of a Clouded Salamander population in southwestern Oregon revealed that four species seemed especially important as prey: an unidentified isopod, a snout beetle, the European earwig and an ant species.

Habitat: Large decaying logs and stumps, particularly of Douglas-fir, are inhabited by Clouded Salamanders when the wood has decayed enough to allow invasion by ants, termites and other invertebrates. These produce burrows that can be used by the salamanders. When the logs or stumps are in earlier stages of decomposition, Clouded Salamanders may be found under loosened slabs of bark. When the wood decay has proceeded to the point of too much drying, the salamanders leave. Old burns and clear-cuts may host large populations of Clouded Salamanders until excess drying of the wood forces them out. Clouded Salamanders also can be found in rock outcrops and road cuts and can retreat deep into available crevices during dry or cold spells. During warm, wet weather, individuals of this species are easy to find under woody surface debris. Clouded Salamanders are capable climbers, probably due to their expanded toe tips and prehensile tail. They have been found at least 61 m up in snags.

Remarks: It is probable that with the passage of time and the advent of cleaner logging methods, appropriate logs and stumps have been decreasing, and that this species is increasingly confined to suitable rock habitats. Until a few years ago, the Clouded Salamander and the Wandering Salamander *(Aneides vagrans)* were considered the same species, but molecular evidence has shown that they are actually two different species. However, they are very difficult, if not impossible, to distinguish on the basis of morphology and color.

BLACK SALAMANDER

Aneides flavipunctatus   STRAUCH

Author: R. Bruce Bury

Description: The coloration of Black Salamanders is highly variable, but most usually have a **black body color overlaid with small, whitish spots or with an infusion of bronze or, more often, olive green. The venter is black or slate.** Body size is moderately large at about 65–75 mm SVL and may reach about 160 mm TL. There are **15–16 costal grooves. This salamander has a prehensile tail. Larger adults have a triangular head** related to enlarged musculature behind the eyes. Juveniles tend to have a greenish sheen on the dorsum, and some appear almost metallic green in coloration. Yellow occurs at the base of limbs, often with many small, white or blue spots.

Variation: There is much local variation in the species. Adults in the northern part of the range retain juvenile-like characteristics: the greenish wash or brassy color and small, white spots. A partial albino was found in California. Animals from southern and inland areas tend to have larger white spots. There are two subspecies, but these are rarely recognized anymore. The center of the geographic range is north of the San Francisco Bay area, where most of the Black Salamanders have 15 costal grooves. Populations north and south of there (isolated in the Santa Cruz Mountains) have 16 or more costal grooves.

Eggs: Our knowledge of clutch size is based on one nest that had 15 eggs. Dissection of females revealed 6–13 large ovarian eggs in one sample and 5–25 in another. Mean clutch size was about 12 eggs. Larger females deposit more eggs per clutch than smaller individuals. Eggs are white, each measuring 5.9–6.4 mm in diameter, and are attached by a 5 mm pedicel to overhanging objects. There is no free-living larval stage; hatchlings are juvenile salamanders.

Similar Species: In southern Oregon, the Black Salamander occurs with three species that may cause confusion in identification: Clouded Salamanders are gray or tan on the venter, and their toe tips have squared toe pads; Del Norte Salamanders have a more slender appearance, 18–19 costal grooves, and either a reddish stripe (especially in juveniles) or a solid brown to black dorsum; and Siskiyou Mountains Salamanders also are slender, have 17–18 costal grooves, and generally have a dark brown dorsum with small, white flecks. In northern California, Black Salamanders occur with several other terrestrial salamanders. The most likely one to cause confusion is the related Arboreal Salamander, which tends to have a uniform tan or brown color and

Adult

Humboldt County, California

WILLIAM LEONARD

Adult

Mendocino County, California

WILLIAM LEONARD

Adult attending eggs

Humboldt County, California

WILLIAM LEONARD

Adult
*Humboldt County,
California*

Adult
*Humboldt County,
California*

Adult
*Santa Cruz County,
California*

a white venter. Arboreal Salamanders reach larger sizes, and adults are stockier than Black Salamanders. Within their small range, Shasta Salamanders may appear similar to Black Salamanders, especially juveniles. Shasta Salamanders can be distinguished by close inspection of their toes, which are webbed along half their toe length.

Distribution: Black Salamanders range from the forested mountains of southernmost Oregon through the Coast Range to Mendocino County, California. They are absent in adjacent Marin County and the San Francisco Bay area but reappear south of San Francisco Bay in the Santa Cruz Mountains and into the Monterey Bay region. Isolated populations occur in the foothills north of Shasta Lake, then along the eastern slopes of the Coast Range southward. They occur from sea level to about 600 m, but a few reach up to 1400 m elevation. Populations occur in areas that receive more than 75 cm of annual precipitation.

Life History: Females likely deposit eggs underground in summer and attend the nest. Animals reach sexual maturity at about 60–75 mm TL.

Natural History: Most of the Black Salamander's diet is invertebrate prey. Larger salamanders consume larger prey. They in turn are preyed upon by gartersnakes, mammals and birds. Black Salamanders exhibit some territorial behavior. In captivity, adults may bite each other, and many animals in the field have scars, suggesting agonistic behavior between individuals. Black Salamanders occur with Ensatina, California Slender, Wandering and Arboreal Salamanders in northern California, and Clouded Salamanders and Ensatina in southern Oregon.

Habitat: Black Salamanders are usually found under downed wood, bark or rocks in the rainy season between October and May. They occupy a wide variety of habitats from sea level to about 1500 m elevation. In northwestern California, Black Salamanders sometimes are found in Redwood stands but appear absent in dense stands closest to the coast. Populations frequent slopes with oaks and conifers such as Douglas-fir, and sometimes they occur in open, dry sites. Black Salamanders flourish in talus slopes. They seem to be restricted to rocky ravines and seeps in more interior locales. In the southern part of its range, this species may be found year-round in seeps or along streams.

Remarks: Black Salamanders have become rarer in recent years, particularly due to the proliferation of vineyards in northern California that has destroyed much of their prime habitat.

ARBOREAL SALAMANDER

Aneides lugubris   HALLOWELL

Author: R. Bruce Bury

Description: Arboreal Salamanders are large, measuring 60–95 mm SVL and 120–190 mm TL. Some adults are hefty compared to other western terrestrial salamanders. Most have **15 costal grooves** and relatively **long legs with long toes free of basal webbing.** The **prehensile tail** often is **held in a curl.** Dorsally, they are light to dark brown with a sheen to the skin and often have many small spots that are yellow to cream in color. The venter is light gray or pale. Arboreal Salamanders often have dull yellow on the underneath of the feet and tail. **Large adults have a triangular-shaped head** due to pronounced jaw musculature behind the eyes. They have large, protruding maxillary teeth that can be felt if one rubs the front of the mouth (but they may bite!).

Young salamanders are dark in coloration, infused with brass or gray, especially on the snout, above the forelimbs and dorsally. Juvenile Arboreal Salamanders may be profusely spotted.

Variation: Arboreal Salamanders in the Monterey Bay region have a high number of dorsal spots. Those in the Sierra Nevada foothills lack or have little spotting and are genetically distinct from coastal populations. Some individual Arboreal Salamanders on Farallon Island west of San Francisco Bay have extensive spotting; they were earlier described as a distinct subspecies, but few experts now recognize this distinction.

Eggs: Clutch size is usually 14–19 eggs (range 5–24). Eggs often are in a cluster and are attached by a 10–20 mm long pedicel to an overhanging object. Individual, whitish eggs are about 7–9.5 mm in diameter and have two jelly envelopes. There is no free-living larval stage; hatchlings are juvenile salamanders.

Similar Species: In northern California, the Arboreal Salamander sometimes occurs with Black or Clouded Salamanders, both of which have gray or dark venters and appear more slender-bodied. Clouded Salamanders have squarish pads on their toe tips, and coloration is often mottled, not so uniform as in Arboreal Salamanders. Black Salamanders have shorter legs and digits and more rounded toe tips. Clouded Salamanders are greener or more brassy in color in the north and black in the south and inland.

Distribution: Arboreal Salamanders range from northern Baja California north through the California Coast Range to central Humboldt County in northwestern California. Isolated populations occur in the Sierra Nevada foothills east of the San Joaquin Valley, California. Arboreal Salamanders occur on several of the larger islands off the California coast.

Adult
*Humboldt County,
California*

WILLIAM LEONARD

Adult
*Alameda County,
California*

WAYNE VAN DEVENDER

Portrait of an adult
*Alameda County,
California*

WAYNE VAN DEVENDER

Adult
Alameda County, California

Adult
Alameda County, California

Life History: Females deposit eggs in June and July in the dry summer period. They coil around the eggs and guard the nest. Males may be present. Incubation takes 3–4 months, and small juveniles hatch in the early fall. Juveniles may take 3 or more years to reach sexual maturity.

Natural History: Arboreal Salamanders are frequently found under branches, downed wood, bark or rocks on the ground in the rainy season between October and May. Arboreal Salamanders occur with California Slender, Wandering, Black and Ensatina Salamanders in northern California. Sometimes they are under the same cover with reptiles such as Northern Alligator Lizards. Arboreal Salamanders are noted for congregating in tree boles or crevices during dry summer periods. They are also known to occur in trees up to about 30 m above the ground. The tail may be used in climbing. Still, they likely spend most of their lives on the ground. Scars on the sides of Arboreal Salamanders suggest aggressive interactions between adults, and adults appear to be territorial in the breeding season. They eat relatively larger prey compared to other terrestrial salamanders in the west, likely due to their relatively larger heads and body size. There are records of California Slender Salamanders in their diet, but most of their food is invertebrates. Predators likely include gartersnakes, rattlesnakes, mammals and birds.

Habitat: Arboreal Salamanders live in live-oak woodland or sometimes in Ponderosa Pine or Black Oak. Some have been found in meadows and openings following clear-cutting of Redwoods in northern California, but Arboreal Salamanders were absent in adjacent old-growth stands. They are able to survive in oak woodland habitats that are hot and dry in summer, but they occur in areas with rain (> 25 cm) at other times of the year.

Remarks: Arboreal Salamanders may emit a squeak when first captured, and large individuals may bite when grabbed. They may reach high densities (about 5000/hectare [2000/acre]) in some areas. This species occurs in drier habitats than most other plethodontid salamanders. As T.I. Storer stated in 1925: "It seems to have gone about as far as a non-aquatic salamander can go in the direction of a terrestrial existence, short of the development of a dermal armor to check loss of moisture."

WANDERING SALAMANDER

Aneides vagrans　　　WAKE AND JACKMAN

Authors: Kristiina Ovaska and Theodore M. Davis

Description: The Wandering Salamander is a medium-sized salamander measuring about 50–110 mm TL. The body is robust for a lungless salamander. The head is broad, somewhat triangular, and jaw musculature is well developed. The limbs and digits are relatively long, except the short, first, inner digit. **The digits are square-ended. The dorsal surface of adults is mottled with black (or dark brown) and gray, which often has a bronze tinge to it.** The underside is translucent gray. Hatchlings are more slender and measure about 13–16 mm SVL (25 mm TL). Their coloration is a lighter bronze or copper color. The triangular-shaped patch on the snout is diagnostic. The upper leg is often the same bronze or copper color, and there are two bronze stripes on the dorsal neck. The back may be similarly bright, giving the appearance of a broad dorsal stripe with irregular edges. The sides are brownish or gray with dark mottling. Older juveniles have intermediate patterns. Very dark individuals with some degree of mottling occur at some localities.

Eggs: The eggs are suspended from the roof of the nesting cavity by long, gelatinous strands. Newly laid eggs are nearly spherical, cream colored and enclosed in two transparent envelopes. Eggs measure about 5–6 mm in diameter, becoming slightly oblong and darker with time. The clutch size ranges from 3–28 (average 12) eggs, based on a small number of field observations. There is no free-living larval stage; hatchlings are juvenile salamanders.

Similar Species: Due to their distinct appearance and coloration, adults of the Wandering Salamander are unlikely to be confused with other salamanders, with the exception of other *Aneides* with overlapping ranges in California. The Black Salamander is larger and has shorter limbs and a black background color. The Arboreal Salamander is much larger and more robust, and the background color is brown, usually with distinct cream to yellow spots. The Wandering Salamander is similar to its sibling species, the Clouded Salamander, but identification usually can be inferred from geographical location, as their ranges have little overlap. Young individuals may be confused with those of Oregon Ensatina, but the latter lacks the coppery patch on the snout and has bright yellow patches on the upper surface of the leg bases. Hatchlings must be examined carefully, however, as juvenile Wandering Salamanders occasionally have yellow leg patches.

Distribution: This species has a disjunct distribution, as it occurs on Vancouver Island (and many of the surrounding small islands) in British

Adult
Vancouver Island,
British Columbia

KRISTIINA OVASKA

Adult
Vancouver Island,
British Columbia

KRISTIINA OVASKA

Juvenile
Vancouver Island,
British Columbia

KRISTIINA OVASKA

Adult
*Humboldt County,
California*

Adult
*Humboldt County,
California*

Adult
*Humboldt County,
California*

Columbia, and in northern California. On Vancouver Island, it occurs at lower elevations (below about 600 m) throughout the island. In California, it is found in coastal forests from northern Siskiyou and Del Norte Counties southward through Humboldt and Trinity Counties to near Stewart's Point, Sonoma County. The species is notably absent from Washington. A sibling species, the Clouded Salamander, occurs in Oregon and extreme northwestern California; the two species co-occur within a narrow (< 15 km wide) zone near Smith River in northwestern California.

Life History: Like other western plethodontids, this species reproduces on land and has direct development (eggs hatch into miniature versions of adults). The female lays her eggs in moist, secluded locations in spring or early summer, and the eggs hatch in early fall. The female usually attends the developing eggs, but on a few occasions, both a male and a female have been found with a clutch within a nesting cavity. Sexual maturity appears to occur at the age of 3 years or more at a body size of about 50 mm SVL. Similar to the Clouded Salamander, males may mature earlier and at a smaller body size than females, but little information is available. Females probably reproduce every other year.

Natural History: The seasonal activity period of the species shows geographic differences. In British Columbia, individuals are most active from spring to fall and retreat to sheltered microhabitats during colder winter months. In California, they are active from fall to spring and estivate during the drier summer months. Individual Wandering Salamanders are site-tenacious and can be found repeatedly in the same location, even from year to year. These salamanders are good climbers and possess morphological specializations for arboreal existence (long digits and enlarged toe pads). It is believed that in Redwood

forests of northern California, at least some individuals complete their life cycle in the canopy without ever descending to the ground. The diet consists of a wide variety of invertebrates. Carpenter ants are an important prey item at some localities. Predators of this salamander are not well known.

Habitat: These salamanders inhabit old- and second-growth coniferous and mixed forests. They are typically found in cavities within decaying logs and stumps or under loose bark in moderately decayed logs. However, the species shows flexibility in habitat use patterns across its range. In Redwood forests of northern California, Wandering Salamanders appear to be highly arboreal. They have been found up to about 90 m in the canopy. On a small, treeless island in British Columbia, they are found under beach logs and in seabird burrows. In addition, some populations exist in urban areas. Most reported nests have been under bark or in cracks within moderately decayed, large logs. One nest was at the base of a branch under an epiphytic fern in a Redwood tree at a height of 30–40 m above the ground.

Remarks: Prior to 1998, the Wandering Salamander was included with the Clouded Salamander as the species *Aneides ferreus*. It is now considered a separate species, based on molecular evidence. At least two hypotheses exist to explain its disjunct distribution. One hypothesis suggests that it was introduced to Vancouver Island from California during the nineteenth century with shipments of Tanoak bark used for tanning leather. This hypothesis is supported by the genetic similarity of the British Columbia and California populations. An alternative hypothesis suggests that the Vancouver Island population survived the last glaciation in refugia. Neither hypothesis is entirely satisfactory, and the issue requires more investigation.

CALIFORNIA SLENDER SALAMANDER

Batrachoseps attenuatus   ESCHSCHOLTZ

Authors: David B. Wake and Shawn R. Kuchta

Description: This species is immediately distinguished from all other salamanders in the region of this book by its **extreme elongation, short limbs and diminutive digits,** and by having only **four toes on the hind limb. The tail is much longer than the head plus body.** Adult body size is somewhat variable and can measure to about 55 mm SVL, yet most individuals are less than 45 mm SVL. There are usually **20 or 21 costal grooves,** counting one each in the axilla and groin, and the **legs fail to overlap, with 11–13 intercostal folds between adpressed limbs.** Sexually active males have somewhat swollen snouts and enlarged premaxillary teeth, but otherwise there is no sexual dimorphism. The ground color is dark gray tending to brown or black, typically with a broad dorsal stripe that is light and bright, yellowish brown or reddish in color. This stripe is bordered by a black lateral stripe. The flanks are gray, heavily spotted with dirty white. The tail is blackish, often with gaps in the pigment so that the underlying fleshy color shows through, giving an impression of an infusion of yellow. The venter is light gray, finely speckled with white.

Variation: There is much individual variation in coloration, with the dorsal stripe ranging in color from the usual reddish brown to red, gray, pinkish gray, tan or dirty yellow. Some individuals, especially in the southern part of the range, either have an obscure stripe or lack one entirely. There is little variation in morphology other than that associated with size. No significant geographic variation has been detected in visible traits, but the species is genetically diverse throughout the range. This variation is currently under investigation.

Eggs: Eggs are relatively large; the white yolks average about 4 mm diameter. Clutch size is from 16–25 eggs, based on clutch sizes observed in the laboratory. In the field, communal clutches seem to be the rule, an exceptional situation for a plethodontid salamander. Females with complete tails lay more eggs than those regrowing tails that have been fully or partly lost. There is no free-living larval stage; hatchlings emerge as juvenile salamanders.

Similar Species: The only salamander in the region of this book that might be confused with the California Slender Salamander is the Oregon Slender Salamander, which occurs in the Cascade Range of central and northern Oregon and differs in being more robust, with a shorter tail and a belly with large, bright white spots on a dark gray to black background. However, their ranges do not overlap. All other salamander species have five toes on the hind foot and are more

Adults
*San Mateo County,
California*

Adult
*San Mateo County,
California*

Underside of an adult
*Del Norte County,
California*

Adult
*Del Norte County,
California*

Adult
*Curry County,
Oregon*

Adult
*Del Norte County,
California*

robust. South of the region included in this book, at the southern end of the species' range in Santa Cruz County, California, this species overlaps with the genetically distinct *Batrachoseps gavilanensis*, a recently described but distantly related form that is morphologically extremely similar, differing mainly in having somewhat larger limbs and in being a bit more attenuated.

Distribution: This species is widespread in northern California, from Santa Cruz, Santa Clara and San Benito Counties in the south through the Coast Range into southwestern Oregon, where it occurs in a narrow strip along the coast as far north as the south side of the Rogue River. From the area north of San Francisco Bay, the range becomes increasingly restricted toward the coast.

Life History: Nothing is known about the courtship behavior of this species. Females typically emerge from underground retreats fully gravid during early fall rains and deposit their eggs in October and November. The eggs are laid in a series connected by a jelly strand which often breaks as the eggs are moved in the chamber. The eggs are deposited in clusters and may or may not be attended by a female. Communal nests often have no adult in attendance. Eggs typically are deposited deep in soil and are rarely encountered. In the laboratory at 13°C, eggs take about 79 days to hatch into miniatures of adults, external gills having been resorbed almost completely before hatching. Females are thought to mature in about 3.5 years, and skeletal aging studies have shown that adults can be at least 8 years old.

Natural History: California Slender Salamanders are semifossorial, spending much of their time underground, and they are most commonly encountered under surface cover such as fallen limbs, logs, pieces of bark and stones. They can be observed readily on moist nights in the spring and fall when they emerge from underground retreats to forage. They do not make their own burrows but rather use cavities produced by rotting roots and cracked soil, as well as burrows made by other animals. Roadside banks are especially good places to observe them while they are foraging. Predation intensity appears to be high, judging by the high frequency of tail loss. Tails are fully regenerated once lost. Sometimes animals are found that have regenerated their tails several different times, as can be seen by the abrupt transitions in size along the tail. California Slenders' primary defenses are remaining motionless or tightly coiling, usually with the head hidden beneath the coil. They may coil and uncoil rapidly and fling themselves about. If the full tail of a female is lost, she will usually forego reproduction that year in favor of regrowing the tail, which is a major fat deposition site. Small arthropods are the dominant prey of California Slender Salamanders. Prey includes springtails, soil mites and tiny centipedes. They capture prey with a remarkably long, very fast tongue.

Habitat: In general, California Slender Salamanders are found in wooded areas or in ecotones at the edges of forest and grassland. They can also be found in coastal scrubland and in chaparral, but in the southern parts of their range, they also occur in open grasslands, where they can be found under isolated trees. These salamanders persist in urban areas and are often encountered in gardens.

Remarks: This is a widespread and common species. In the central and southern portions of its range, it can reach very high densities. In the northern parts of its range in extreme northwestern California and Oregon, it is generally uncommon.

OREGON SLENDER SALAMANDER

Batrachoseps wrighti ·   BISHOP

Author: Robert M. Storm

Description: This is a medium-sized salamander measuring from about 40 mm SVL to 64 mm SVL and from 90 mm TL to 118 mm TL. Like all other slender salamanders, it has a long, slim body form, with 16–17 costal grooves, and a long tail, which can be 1.0–1.75 times its body length. It usually **has a dorsal, reddish brown or chestnut, uneven-edged stripe extending to the end of its tail.** The sides are dark brown to black and are speckled with small, white, bluish white or silvery flecks. **The ventral side of the body and tail is black, with conspicuous larger, white flecks scattered throughout.** The Oregon Slender Salamander has relatively short legs (4.5–7.5 intercostal folds between adpressed limbs) and small front and rear feet, and **there**

are only four toes on the back feet. Hatchlings are 19–35 mm TL and have a stouter appearance, with relatively longer legs and shorter tails than adults.

Variation: Individuals with gold or greenish gold stripes on their backs often occur in the Columbia Gorge.

Eggs: There are few records of finding eggs of this species in the field, as they are probably placed deep in decaying logs or stumps, or below the ground surface in spaces within rock outcrops or talus. From ovarian egg counts, clutches range from 3–11 eggs. The eggs measure about 4 mm in diameter, are cream in color and are strung together by gelatinous strands that are extensions of the gel around each egg. The eggs are rather like beads on a string spaced about 20 mm apart. There is no free-living larval stage; hatchlings emerge as juvenile salamanders.

Similar Species: No other species in the range of the Oregon Slender Salamander displays a combination of four toes per hind foot and a ventral side that is slate black with large, white flecks.

Distribution: This species occurs only in Oregon and occupies the forested west slopes of the Cascade Range from the Columbia River to southern Lane County. Within this north-south range extent of about 240 km, the species is not homogeneously distributed but appears to occur at disjunct locations. At this time, less than 200 discrete sites are known for this species. It has been found from 15 m elevation at the Columbia River Gorge to 1430 m elevation toward the south of its range. Near Mount Hood, the range extends east of the Cascade Range crest into Wasco County at a few scattered sites.

Life History: Courtship probably occurs during warm, rainy periods in the late fall and early spring. The eggs are deposited at some time during the spring. Females have been found with eggs, but it is not known

Adult
*Lane County,
Oregon*

BRAD MOON

Adult
*Wasco County,
Oregon*

BRAD MOON

Adult
*Marion County,
Oregon*

ROBERT M. STORM

Adult
*Lane County,
Oregon*

Adult
*Marion County,
Oregon*

Adult
*Linn County,
Oregon*

if parental care is involved. The eggs have a long incubation period, hatching in 4 or 5 months. Time to maturity and longevity are unknown.

Natural History: Several individuals of this species are often found clumped together under the same object. When uncovered, the salamanders often assume a tight spiral and, if further disturbed, may flip about violently. This may be a possible deterrent to predators. The tail breaks off easily if seized. In one study, this species was found to have eaten a variety of small insects and other invertebrates, including springtails, mites, flies, spiders, snails, beetles, centipedes and earthworms.

Habitat: The Oregon Slender Salamander is most common in evergreen forests with moist microhabitat conditions and large, downed wood. It can occur in second growth, but it is an "old-growth associate," meaning it consistently has been found in higher abundances in mature and older forests, compared to younger managed stands (0–80 years of age). Oregon Slender Salamanders can be found beneath the bark or within the termite channels of large, old logs and stumps. In warm, wet weather, individuals may be found under debris on the surface of the ground (pieces of bark, limbs, etc.). They also have been found under large, moss-covered rocks in the Columbia River Gorge area and in stabilized talus elsewhere. In one study, this species frequented decaying logs and surface debris on an exposed lava flow in the vicinity of Santiam Pass in central Oregon. It is probable that these salamanders use the crevices of the lava for shelter and reproduction.

Remarks: This is the only salamander endemic to Oregon. Three discrete populations, occurring in a north-south latitudinal gradient, have been identified using genetic techniques. Three species management units were proposed to preserve this genetic diversity, apparently a consequence of isolated populations due to the limited dispersal capabilities of this terrestrial salamander. Field research has shown that the Oregon Slender Salamander appears to prefer older and larger types of woody debris, the types most often associated with unmanaged forests. Harvesting of these forests is likely to reduce the overall abundance of this microhabitat type, as large, downed wood recruitment is not a managed commodity across the forest landscape. Declines of this species within the managed forest landscape of the western Cascade Range are a concern, especially at lower to mid-elevation sites, which may provide optimal habitat for this species.

ENSATINA

Ensatina eschscholtzii   GRAY

Authors: Shawn R. Kuchta and David B. Wake

Description: The Ensatina is a medium-sized salamander with a **short, robust torso (12–13 costal grooves) and long legs. Toes overlap when the legs are adpressed.** Adult body sizes vary geographically, averaging 50–60 mm SVL. The tails of males are slender and typically a bit longer than the head plus body length; females possess relatively short, stocky tails that are slightly shorter than the torso. **A feature unique to Ensatina is the constriction at the base of the tail, just posterior to the cloaca. There is no dorsal stripe. The proximal limb segments are yellow to orange** and contrast with the dorsal coloration.

Variation: Three of the seven subspecies of Ensatina occur within the range of this field guide. The Oregon Ensatina *(Ensatina eschscholtzii oregonensis)* is light to dark brown dorsally and fleshy-pale on the

belly, with a fine stippling of black specks. The upper eyelids match the dorsal coloration. Proximal limb segments are yellow to yellow-orange. There is a light speckling of yellow in the eye. Juveniles are similar to adults but often exhibit black mottling on the back or are covered in light-colored flecks. The proximal limb segment in juveniles is bright yellow or orange, but the constriction at the base of the tail is more subtle. The Painted Ensatina *(E. e. picta)* is very similar to the Oregon Ensatina but with a mottling of small, yellow to orange and black splotches on the back and tail. Often, streaks of black are present along the dorsolateral parts of the trunk. The Yellow-eyed Ensatina *(E. e. xanthoptica)* has a dark brown back, orange proximal limb segments, usually orange upper eyelids, solid orange belly and a bold yellow eye patch above and below the iris. Juveniles resemble adults.

The subspecies designation of the Painted Ensatina is disputed. It may be best regarded as a local color polymorphism of the Oregon Ensatina because it is not genetically distinct, and within its range, individuals can be found that are colored like Oregon Ensatina. The striped pattern can be found as a variant color pattern as far north as central Oregon. The Yellow-eyed Ensatina, on the other hand, is highly differentiated from the Oregon Ensatina, both genetically and in color pattern. Within the Yellow-eyed Ensatina subspecies, populations from the region east and north of San Francisco Bay are genetically distinct from populations south and west of the Bay region, and individuals have more vivid coloration. In northern California, the Oregon Ensatina shows strong geographic variation with respect to genetic traits. In contrast, Oregon Ensatinas in Washington and Oregon are relatively weakly differentiated. Where subspecies meet, they intergrade in color pattern.

Adult
*Clark County,
Washington*

WILLIAM LEONARD

Adult
*Curry County,
Oregon*

WILLIAM LEONARD

Adult
*Humboldt County,
California*

CHARLES M. CRISAFULLI

Adult
*Sonoma County,
California*

WILLIAM LEONARD

Juvenile
*Thurston County,
Washington*

WILLIAM LEONARD

**An adult Yellow-eyed
Ensatina in defensive
posture**
*Santa Cruz County,
California*

WILLIAM LEONARD

Eggs: Eggs range from 5.0–7.8 mm in diameter, including the ova and two jelly coats. Ova are solid white to cream. They are laid in globular clusters of up to 25 eggs (9–16 being most common) and stick together but are not connected by jelly cords. Like many plethodontids, females attend the eggs until hatching, and identification of the attending female is probably the easiest way to identify Ensatina eggs. Eggs are rarely found. There is no free-living larval stage; hatchlings emerge as juvenile salamanders.

Similar Species: No other western salamander species has the constricted tail base. Adpressed limbs overlap in Ensatina, unlike in woodland salamanders (*Plethodon*) and slender salamanders (*Batrachoseps*). The Long-toed Salamander has a dorsal stripe and a longer fourth toe on the hind foot. The Northwestern and Tiger Salamanders are larger and lack nasolabial grooves (a feature of the family Plethodontidae, to which Ensatina belongs). The Northwestern Salamander has highly developed parotoid glands. The Clouded and Arboreal Salamanders have squared-off toe tips and prehensile tails, and the Black Salamander has a black belly and shorter toes. Juvenile Ensatinas may appear similar to Shasta Salamanders, but the webbed toes of the Shasta should be apparent.

Distribution: This is the most wide-spread West Coast salamander, ranging from central coastal British Columbia, Canada, to northern Baja California, Mexico. In Washington, Oregon and northern California, it principally is found in forests west of the Cascade Crest, up to an elevation of about 1400 m (the species is most common below about 915 m). In central California, it is encountered west of the Central Valley in the coastal ranges and along the western slopes of the Sierra Nevada.

Life History: Ensatinas mate from the fall through spring. Eggs are laid in the late spring and early summer. They develop over the summer, hatching in the fall. Ensatinas mature at 3–4 years old and can live up to 15 years.

Natural History: Courtship involves an elaborate "dance" that lasts for hours and that ends when the male places a spermatophore on the forest floor and the female picks it up with her cloaca. Females deposit fertilized eggs in secluded, moist microhabitats, such as in logs, root channels and animal burrows. Adults and juveniles become active with the fall rains. Ensatinas possess anti-predator defenses. The skin and tail contain poison glands, and harassed Ensatinas will exude a sticky, white toxin. If the situation is life threatening, an Ensatina can voluntarily lose its tail, which breaks off at the constriction. The tail thrashes wildly about, attracting the attention of predators while the Ensatina sneaks away. It takes about 2 years for an Ensatina to regenerate a lost tail.

Habitat: Ensatinas are broadly distributed among coniferous and deciduous forests. They never enter water but do require moist microhabitats. While the forest remains moist, they can be found under rocks and logs and in talus, leaf litter, piles of bark and even backyard wood piles. During the dry summer months, they retreat to cool, moist microhabitats, usually underground.

Remarks: Seven subspecies are recognized, three of which occur in the Pacific Northwest. Subspecies vary greatly in genetics and color pattern, and the complex has been important in studying the evolution of species. The Painted Ensatina and the Oregon Ensatina color patterns are thought to reduce predation by virtue of crypsis. In contrast, the Yellow-eyed Ensatina is thought to mimic newts (genus *Taricha*), which are extremely toxic.

SHASTA SALAMANDER

Hydromantes shastae   GORMAN AND CAMP

Author: Deanna H. Olson

Description: Salamanders of the genus *Hydromantes* are the "web-toed" salamanders. In the northwestern region, Shasta Salamanders are easily distinguished from other plethodontids by their **webbed toes, with webbing along half of the toe length, somewhat flattened body and head,** and a blunt, cylindrical tail that extends about one-third of their body length. They have **13 costal grooves.** They are **relatively long-limbed: adult adpressed limbs overlap by 0.5 to 1.5 intercostal folds; juvenile limb overlap may be up to 2.5–3 intercostal folds.** Shasta Salamanders measure from about 23 mm TL at hatching to 100 mm TL (SVL to 87 mm). One-year-olds are about 46 mm TL. Dorsal colors are intermixed in a speckled or mottled pattern and may be gray, green, beige, tan or reddish. The tail usually has some yellow. Ventral color includes white blotches, with silver flecking on the sides, lower limbs and feet of adults.

Variation: Shasta Salamanders are genetically diverse. There is as much genetic variation within the Shasta Salamander species complex as that recorded among all three California species of *Hydromantes*.

Eggs: Grapelike clusters of 9 eggs, attended by females, have been reported in cave crevices. Eggs develop directly into juvenile salamanders; there is no free-living larval stage.

Similar Species: Shasta Salamanders may occur with Ensatinas (distinguished by tail constriction and a yellow to white ventral coloration) and Black Salamanders (which exhibit no limb overlap when adpressed and which have black dorsal and dark gray ventral coloration). Upon close inspection, the webbed toes of Shasta Salamanders should distinguish them. In particular, juvenile Shasta Salamanders potentially can be mistaken for one of these other species, especially Black Salamanders, which also have greenish juveniles. The webbed toes are the best way to distinguish the two, and Black Salamanders have more costal grooves (14–16). Ensatina juveniles may not be readily distinguished because their coloration varies, and they may appear similar to Shasta Salamanders: they may have 12–13 costal grooves, and the constriction at the base of the tail may be difficult to see.

Distribution: Shasta Salamanders occur near Shasta Lake, California. Currently, 61 sites are documented in a patchy distribution, representing about 16 to 17 population centers. In a north-south direction, sites occur across about a 50 km area from near the southern tip of Lake McCloud to about 7 km south of Shasta Lake. The east-west range extends almost 40 km, with western-most sites within 2–3 km of Shasta Lake and eastern sites about 8 km from Shasta

Adult and young
*Shasta County,
California*

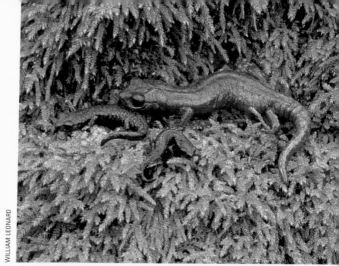

WILLIAM LEONARD

Adult
*Shasta County,
California*

WILLIAM LEONARD

Portrait of an adult
*Shasta County,
California*

WILLIAM LEONARD

Adult

Shasta County, California

Adult

Shasta County, California

Juvenile

Shasta County, California

Lake near Highway 299. Maximum recorded elevation for this species is 975 m.

Life History: Little is known about Shasta Salamander reproduction, but it is assumed to follow the general plethodontid pattern of internal fertilization via male spermatophore. Males in breeding condition have been reported in September, gravid females have been observed in the spring, and oviposition occurs in the summer. Females brood eggs, curling around them, presumably to prevent desiccation, disease and predation. Eggs hatch in late fall, and hatchlings can be found at the ground surface after the onset of wet conditions.

Natural History: Shasta Salamanders can be found on the surface during restricted microclimate conditions. Generally, they may be found during fall, winter and spring rains. At rock outcrops, they have been found when temperatures were 3.9–11.7°C and relative humidity ranged from 75–100%. Their diet consists of small invertebrates. Predators may include snakes and shrews. Population sizes are not known. The size of habitat areas associated with particular populations has been estimated to range from less than 0.4 ha to 6300 ha.

Habitat: Although historically this salamander was described as a habitat specialist, occurring in association with limestone rock outcrops, it is now also known from volcanic rock outcrops, meta-sedimentary rock talus, and areas with only scattered surface rock. Shasta Salamanders occur in caves, cracks and crevices of outcrops, under rocks on outcrops and in road cuts. Adjacent to limestone outcrops, they have been found under surface debris, primarily downed wood, up to 200 m from surface rock. Vegetation at sites is variable, including Douglas-fir, Gray Pine, Black Oak, Knobcone Pine, Bigleaf Maple, Canyon Live Oak, Mountain Mahogany, Douglas Maple, California Hazel, Wild Currant, Thimbleberry, California Buckeye, Honeysuckle, Redberry, Poison Oak, Maidenhair Fern, moss and grass.

Remarks: The global distribution of the genus *Hydromantes* is disjunct. It is the only plethodontid salamander group occurring in both the Old and New Worlds. In California, there are three species, with two species occurring further south in the Sierra Nevada. Other *Hydromantes* are known only from southern Europe, where seven species are described having similarly restricted distributions in southern France, Italy and Sardinia. Web-toed salamanders are adept climbers, aided by their flattened body, webbed toes and tail. Their tongues are long and may extend to one-third or more of their SVL. The Shasta Salamander was first found by Eustace L. Furlong in the early 1900s but was not described until it was rediscovered many years later by Joseph Gorman. The Shasta Salamander is a California State Threatened Species and is classified as Rare by the International Union for the Conservation of Nature. It has been managed under a U.S. Forest Service comprehensive species management plan since 1979, and under the Survey and Manage Provision of the federal Northwest Forest Plan, 1994 to 2004. Due to genetic diversity within the species, population-specific management plans have been proposed. Two past land management activities have impacted Shasta Salamanders: inundation of habitat by creation of Shasta Dam (about 9500 hectares were flooded) in 1949; and mining of limestone for cement, sugar refining and road-base material. Mining continues to be a primary concern, as do road building, timber harvest and recreation, including cave use and firewood collection.

SCOTT BAR SALAMANDER

Plethodon asupak   MEAD

Authors: Louise S. Mead, Richard S. Nauman and David Clayton

Description: The Scott Bar Salamander is a **long-bodied woodland salamander with a larger head, longer limbs and fewer costal grooves than the Del Norte and Siskiyou Mountains Salamanders.** An adult *Plethodon asupak* has **16–17 costal grooves and 2–3 intercostal folds between adpressed limbs.** These salamanders are chocolate brown to purplish brown and usually possess varying amounts of white to yellowish flecking on the head, sides, dorsum and limbs; males and juveniles may also possess a red dorsal stripe.

Variation: Little is known about any potential variation in this species.

Eggs: While no nests of this species have been found, it may be that they are similar to other western plethodontids. There is no free-living larval stage; hatchlings emerge as juvenile salamanders.

Similar Species: The Del Norte Salamander has a longer body, with 6.5–7.5 intercostal folds between adpressed limbs. The Siskiyou Mountains Salamander has 4–5.5 intercostal folds between adpressed limbs, and juveniles have a brown dorsal stripe. The Black Salamander has a black ground color with a profuse green to bronze wash along the sides of the animal, 3–5 intercostal folds between adpressed limbs and a triangular head. The juveniles of all these species may be difficult to distinguish in the field.

Distribution: The Scott Bar Salamander occurs only in northern Siskiyou County, California, in the Scott River area, from just east of Seiad Valley to Scott Bar Mountain. To date, there are less than ten localities known for the species, although other locations are suspected.

Life History: Little is known about the life history of this new species.

Natural History: These animals are active near the surface during warm and wet periods, usually during the spring when overnight temperatures are above freezing. Because the habitat in the range of this species is very dry, animals may be difficult to find near the surface in any given year.

Habitat: Little is known about the habitat requirements of the species, but it is usually found in association with rocky substrates and in a variety of forested conditions.

Remarks: This species was first collected approximately ten years ago; ongoing genetic and morphological work recently confirmed it as a species separate from the Siskiyou and Del Norte Salamanders. The U.S. Fish and Wildlife Service was recently petitioned to list the Scott Bar Salamander under the Endangered Species Act. Its tiny range is the smallest of any northwestern amphibian.

RICHARD S. NAUMAN

Adult Scott Bar Salamander
Siskiyou County, California

Adult Scott Bar Salamander
Siskiyou County, California

STEPHEN G. TILLEY

DUNN'S SALAMANDER

Plethodon dunni   BISHOP

Author: Robert M. Storm

Description: This is the largest of our northwestern salamanders in the genus *Plethodon*. Adults may measure to 75 mm SVL and 154 mm TL. Dunn's Salamanders usually have **15 costal grooves, with 2–4 intercostal folds between the toes of the adpressed limbs.** Typically, these salamanders have **a yellowish to olive green or tan dorsal stripe that does not quite reach the end of the tail.** The **stripe has uneven edges** and may be rather heavily mottled with black. The sides of the body are dark brown or black and are usually sprinkled with blotches of the same color as the dorsal stripe. Ventral coloration is slate gray with yellow flecks. Males are slightly smaller than females, have longer tails and wider heads, and have a small lobe on each side of the vent. Young individuals

have a brighter, more even-edged dorsal stripe. Hatchlings measure about 16 mm SVL. As do all plethodontids, Dunn's Salamander has a nasolabial groove.

Variation: A melanistic (unstriped) form, briefly considered to be a separate species, *P. gordoni*, is found in the central Oregon Coast Range and is a variant of Dunn's Salamander.

Eggs: Only two nests have been found in the field. One consisted of a grape-like cluster of 9 eggs about 40 mm deep in a crevice in shale rock. The other was a cluster of 12 eggs with an adult coiled around it in a decayed log on the bank of a small stream. Ovarian egg counts range from 4–15 eggs. Mature eggs are yellow and about 5 mm in diameter. There is no free-living larval stage; hatchlings emerge as juvenile salamanders.

Similar Species: The dark phase of Van Dyke's Salamander has a dorsal stripe that extends nearly to the tip of the tail, fewer costal grooves, parotoid glands (which may be inconspicuous) and a yellow throat. The Western Red-backed Salamander has an even-edged stripe that extends to the end of the tail and lacks large blotches of dorsal stripe color on the sides. Dunn's Salamanders of the melanistic form may be difficult to distinguish from melanistic forms of the Western Red-backed Salamander. In particular, hatchlings and small juveniles may be difficult to distinguish. The Larch Mountain Salamander has a pinkish belly. Adult Del Norte Salamanders have no dorsal stripe and show 6.5–7.5 intercostal folds between adpressed limbs. The Long-toed Salamander has longer toes and lacks a nasolabial groove.

Distribution: Dunn's Salamanders are found west of the Cascade Range crest from extreme northwestern California (Del Norte County) to southern Washington. In Washington, this species is found only in the Willapa Hills in the extreme southwestern

Adult
*Pacific County,
Washington*

BRAD MOON

Melanistic adult
*Mary's Peak,
Benton County,
Oregon*

WILLIAM LEONARD

Adult
*Multnomah County,
Oregon*

WILLIAM LEONARD

Dunn's (left) and Van Dyke's (right) Salamanders

Pacific County, Washington

Portrait of an adult

Pacific County, Washington

WILLIAM LEONARD

WILLIAM LEONARD

portion of the state. Dunn's Salamander is increasingly restricted coastward in the Siskiyou Mountains of southwestern Oregon. This species is absent from most of the Willamette Valley, probably due to the absence of rocks and cold streams. Dunn's Salamanders are found from sea level to 1006 m on Mary's Peak, Oregon, and to 610 m in Washington's Willapa Hills.

Life History: Little is known of the breeding habits of Dunn's Salamander. Courtship probably occurs in late fall or in the spring, based on the findings of spermatophore remnants in the cloacae of females. The young go through their larval period in the egg and hatch in about 70 days. They can be found at the surface after fall rains in October and November.

Natural History: In some streamside areas, Dunn's Salamanders can be found year-round, likely due to the moderating influence of the stream on bank micro-climate conditions. They retreat subsurface during freezing or drought conditions and appear to be most active at the surface in April. They often occur along streams inhabited by torrent salamanders and Pacific giant salamanders, and seem to have complementary streamside distributions with Western Red-backed Salamanders. Known predators include Coastal Giant Salamander, American Dipper, Steller's Jay and Northwestern Gartersnake, and they likely are eaten by other birds and small mammals. Springtails are a dominant prey of Dunn's Salamanders, but these salamanders also eat other invertebrates and have been reported to be cannibalistic.

Habitat: Dunn's Salamander is almost always associated with rocks in cool, moist places. It has been characterized as a western forest, stream bank associate. It often occurs within a few meters of small streams within forested landscapes. In the Coast Range, it occurs in outcrops of fine-grained sandstone or shale close to swift-flowing rocky streams. In the Cascade Range, it inhabits stabilized basalt talus, again near water. It may also be found under woody debris, moss or other cover at the edge of streams in cool habitats. Dunn's Salamanders also have been found upslope, away from stream channels. It is probable that they may wander on the forest floor during rainy nights in the wet season, taking cover in moist microhabitats, such as under forest duff or downed wood, during the day.

Remarks: Dunn's Salamander is relatively rare in Washington. In searching for this salamander, one should be careful to replace cover objects as they were after exposing an animal. The removal of tree cover adjacent to mountain streams may cause a temperature increase that is harmful to these salamanders.

DEL NORTE SALAMANDER

Plethodon elongatus   VAN DENBURGH

Author: Hartwell H. Welsh, Jr.

Description: This slender, elegant, **long-bodied salamander has a brown to black ground color on the dorsum, either with or without a brown, red or copper colored stripe, which when present becomes less distinct with age. Its toes are short and slightly webbed. The elongate body has 6.5–7.5 intercostal folds between adpressed limbs.** Size ranges 46–68 mm SVL for mature males and 57–71 mm SVL for mature females. For both genders, TL can be nearly double the SVL if the animals retain a complete (unregenerated) tail. Juveniles show a reddish or copper dorsal stripe from the nose to the tip of the tail, often suffused with dark pigment along its central axis. Juveniles are 21–28.5 mm TL.

Variation: Animals lacking dorsal stripes are common near the coast, becoming less common inland. Recent genetic analyses indicate that the Del Norte Salamander is composed of several distinct lineages. Two divergent lineages occur at the southern end of the range in the lower Klamath and Trinity River Basins, California; both are distinct from populations north of Humboldt County, California. The relationships among these entities and Siskiyou Mountains Salamander, which also appears to consist of more than one genetically distinct lineage, are under investigation, and it is likely that more species in this complex of closely related salamanders will be described in the near future.

Eggs: Only one nest has been found: a subterranean nest with 10 eggs in a grape-like cluster was found at the base of a Redwood fence post. This is probably an atypical site, given the association of this species with rocky substrates. Typical nest sites are probably subterranean cavities associated with unconsolidated talus and other hard substrates. A sample of 18 mature females had an average of 7 large eggs (range of 3–11). This species undergoes direct development in the egg (no free-living larvae); hatchlings emerge as juvenile salamanders.

Similar Species: Dunn's Salamander has a greenish dorsal stripe and has 1–4 intercostal folds between adpressed limbs. The Western Red-backed Salamander is smaller (64 mm SVL) and has 3.5–4.5 intercostal folds between adpressed limbs. The Siskiyou Mountains Salamander has 4–5.5 intercostal folds between adpressed limbs and has a lighter brown dorsal color with abundant light flecking. The Black Salamander has a black background with either small, white to yellow spots or irregular green flecks on the dorsum and sides, and has a triangular head. Ensatina has 12–13 costal grooves and a "swollen" tail, constricted

Adult and juvenile
Humboldt County, California

Juvenile
Humboldt County, California

Adult
Humboldt County, California

Juvenile
Humboldt County, California

at its base. Juvenile Ensatinas have distinct yellow upper arms. Juvenile plethodontids may be difficult to distinguish.

Distribution: The Del Norte Salamander is found in the Klamath-Siskiyou region of northwestern California and southwestern Oregon. In California, it ranges from south-central Humboldt County eastward, just into Trinity County, and from western Siskiyou County to the vicinity of Indian Creek, and northward through Del Norte County. In Oregon, it occurs along the coast (Curry and southernmost Coos Counties) and eastward in the Siskiyou Mountains (Josephine County) to West Cow Creek in the Umpqua River watershed. The range measures 335 km from north to south and extends about 130 km inland. The Del Norte Salamander is found from about sea level to 1700 m above sea level.

Life History: Reproduction is terrestrial. Breeding has not been observed but probably occurs in both spring and fall on the forest floor when surface activity peaks during cool, moist conditions. Parental care is undocumented, but females likely remain with their eggs, as is the case with many species of plethodontid salamanders.

Natural History: The size of this species' home range is not known, but Del Norte Salamanders are highly sedentary, rarely moving more than a few meters in a year (maximum recorded over a 3-year study was 7.5 m). It is not known if they defend territories, but it is likely they defend foraging and retreat sites from other salamanders. Generally, Del Norte Salamanders are far underground during hot summer months and become inactive in cold weather. They are active on the surface only at night and can be found near or on the surface only when air temperatures are 4.5–25°C, soil temperatures are 4.5–20°C, and the relative humidity is 45% or greater. They are sit-and-wait predators that dart out from cover to seize small prey

such as springtails, termites, mites and beetles. They are likely prey for shrews, gartersnakes and other carnivores.

Habitat: This animal is a close associate of older forest conditions in the Pacific Northwest. It is usually associated with talus or rocky substrates, but it can also be found in association with downed woody debris in areas with nearby rock substrates. A forest canopy closure of 60% or greater in mature to late seral forest is the norm to support populations, except in marine-influenced coastal areas, where talus is the primary predictor of occurrence. Juvenile habitat requirements are the same as for adults.

Remarks: The Del Norte Salamander may be declining due to timber harvesting, especially in non-reserve interior locales. Prior to June 2002, this species was afforded some protection on federal forestlands under the Survey and Manage Provision of the Northwest Forest Plan, where ground-disturbing activities were restricted on occupied sites. Currently, it is a Species of Special Concern in California, an administrative category with no real protections afforded. It is a Sensitive Species in Oregon, which affords minimum take limits per day. There are currently no species-specific protections that apply on federal lands. Species management considerations for this endemic salamander include susceptibility to losses from timber harvest that vary by location (risk is higher throughout the largely interior range, especially on south-tending aspects, but lower along the marine-influenced coast). Concern for the loss of local populations is especially important in the areas of divergent genetic lineages (primarily interior Humboldt County, California). The role of reserve lands in these areas is critical for populations to persist.

COEUR D'ALENE SALAMANDER

Plethodon idahoensis SLATER AND SLIPP

Author: Albert G. Wilson, Jr.

Description: The Coeur d'Alene Salamander is a **dark brown or black salamander with a pale yellow dorsal stripe.** The stripe typically has scalloped margins, is usually overlaid with brown on the head and does not reach the tail tip. White or gray flecks occur on legs, sides and belly. Typically, the **chin has an irregular yellow patch.** This is a broad-headed woodland salamander with a relatively short trunk and long legs. It has **parotoid glands and short, slightly webbed toes.** There are typically **14 costal grooves.** Adults measure 45–65 mm SVL and can exceed 100 mm TL. Mature males have nasolabial cirri and lobes on the posterior margin of the vent. Females are slightly larger than males. The coloration

and markings of juvenile Coeur d'Alene Salamanders resemble those of adults. Hatchlings average 18 mm SVL.

Variation: Dorsal stripe color can be green, red or orange. Rarely, melanistic Coeur d'Alene Salamanders with poorly developed dorsal stripes are found. Individuals with red and orange stripes are commonly encountered in the Kootenai Valley of Montana. Dark flecks may occur in the dorsal stripe and yellow chin patch. The chin patch may be fragmented or absent. White flecks vary considerably in size and may sometimes be absent from the legs or body.

Eggs: Coeur d'Alene Salamander nests have not been found in the wild. Eggs observed in captivity were cream colored, averaged 5.0 mm in diameter and were deposited in a gelatinous mass typical of woodland salamanders. Gravid females bear an average of 6 eggs and probably suspend the egg mass from rocks or the walls of crevices. There is no free-living larval stage; hatchlings emerge as juvenile salamanders.

Similar Species: The Long-toed Salamander is commonly mistaken for the Coeur d'Alene Salamander, but the former has longer toes and lacks a yellow chin patch, nasolabial grooves and parotoid glands. The Coeur d'Alene Salamander's body proportions and coloration are very similar to those of non-sympatric, dark-phase Van Dyke's Salamanders. Coeur d'Alene Salamanders, however, have a wider head and are more dorsoventrally flattened. They also have a narrower dorsal stripe and more invasion of dark pigment in the dorsal stripe and chin patch than do Van Dyke's Salamanders.

Distribution: The Coeur d'Alene Salamander is the only woodland salamander of the northern Rocky Mountains. Coeur d'Alene Salamanders have been found in mountainous regions, from 500–1550 m elevation. The species

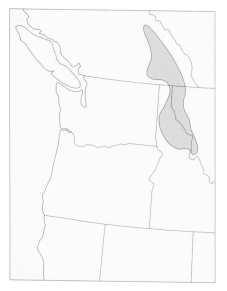

Adult and juvenile
*Kootenai County,
Idaho*

Adult
*Idaho County,
Idaho*

Adult
*Kootenai County,
Idaho*

Adult
Kootenai County, Idaho

Underside of adult
Kootenai County, Idaho

Adult
Idaho County, Idaho

ranges from the Duncan and Columbia River drainages of British Columbia south to the Selkirk River drainage of Idaho and Bitterroot River drainage of Montana. Most known localities where this species is found are in canyons on the west slope of the Bitterroot Range in the Idaho panhandle. Recent surveys have greatly expanded the known range of the Coeur d'Alene Salamander in British Columbia. Its occurrence in the Columbia River drainage indicates that this species may eventually be encountered in northeastern Washington.

Life History: Courtship is similar to that of other woodland salamanders and can be observed on wet nights by flashlight in the spring, late summer and fall. Females lay eggs in alternate years during April and May. Those mating in August may therefore store sperm nine months. Hatchlings can be encountered in October. Coeur d'Alene Salamanders are slow growing and do not sexually mature until their fourth year.

Natural History: Coeur d'Alene Salamanders are nocturnal and take shelter under surface debris or in crevices during the day. They are most active during damp weather above 4.4°C. Cold winters and dry summers in the northern Rocky Mountains force many populations deep underground, and these may emerge for only brief periods in spring and fall to mate and forage. Coeur d'Alene Salamanders are opportunistic predators and eat a variety of invertebrates. Flies and springtails are important prey. Coeur d'Alene Salamanders will enter shallow water and take aquatic prey such as caddis flies and stoneflies. Recorded predators include Red-sided Gartersnakes and American Robins. The salamanders are probably eaten by other birds and possibly by predatory beetles.

Habitat: Coeur d'Alene Salamanders are most common in temperate, moist, coniferous forests of Western Red Cedar and Douglas-fir. These forests comprise a disjunct maritime province in the Rockies that is also home to Rocky Mountain Tailed Frogs and Idaho Giant Salamanders. Coeur d'Alene Salamanders are typically encountered along steep streams and in waterfall spray zones and seepages. They will sometimes enter water to avoid capture. Because of the harsh climate and recurrent wildfires of the Rocky Mountains, populations are associated with deep underground refugia such as talus or rock crevices. Where there is cool surface water, populations may be surface-active throughout the summer. The easiest and least invasive way to observe Coeur d'Alene Salamanders is to look for them at night in roadside fracture seepages.

Remarks: The Coeur d'Alene Salamander was originally described in 1940 as a distinct species, but it subsequently was considered by some to be either a subspecies or an unnamed geographic group of Van Dyke's Salamander. Studies over the last decade support recognition of species status for the Coeur d'Alene Salamander, but some of the important older literature pertinent to this species refers to it as either *Plethodon vandykei idahoensis* or *Plethodon vandykei.*

LARCH MOUNTAIN SALAMANDER

Plethodon larselli   BURNS

Author: Charles M. Crisafulli

Description: The Larch Mountain Salamander is the smallest western *Plethodon*. Adults measure 39–57 mm SVL and up to 105 mm TL. **They have 14–16 costal grooves (modal number = 15). Males lack a mental gland. The outer toe on the hind foot is reduced (single phalanx),** and parotoid glands are indistinct. The **uneven-edged dorsal stripe is red, orange, brown or chestnut** and begins abruptly at the back of the head and continues to the tip of the tail, where it is brightest. Melanophores (black spots) are present in the center of the dorsal stripe, often appearing in a herringbone pattern, but can be so profuse they obscure the dorsal stripe. Melanophores rarely extend to the tail. Stripe color occurs as small flecks on the dorsal surface of the legs and feet. The

sides have a black ground color that shows as a narrow, 1–2 mm wide band extending down from the dorsal stripe. **Below this black band, the sides are profusely dotted with very small, white and gold flecks, giving the lateral surface a "frosted" appearance.** The ventral surface is usually colored orange or red but can be whitish gray. Juveniles differ from adults by having an even-edged dorsal stripe margin that extends from the snout to the tip of the tail with few or no melanophores, and a black venter with single or multiple patches of red-orange.

Variation: The Larch Mountain Salamander has considerable variation in color, both across its range and within populations. Animals captured at the same location may have red, orange, chestnut, brown or an indistinguishable dorsal stripe. Ventral color ranges from bright red to whitish. There is considerable genetic variation among populations of the Larch Mountain Salamander. These genetic differences are greatest between Oregon and Washington populations, suggesting that the Columbia River has been a barrier to gene flow. For conservation purposes, it has been suggested that the Oregon and Washington populations be treated as distinct management units.

Eggs: No nest has been found for this species. Clutch size is likely about 7 eggs. There is no free-living larval stage; hatchlings emerge as juvenile salamanders.

Similar Species: The Western Red-backed Salamander has an even-edged dorsal stripe (with few melanophores) that extends from snout to tip of tail, gray to black venter with large, white flecking, lateral surface with a broad (2–4 mm), black band, and a longer outer toe on the hind foot. Van Dyke's Salamander has a yellow chin patch, parotoid glands and longer outer hind toe. Dunn's Salamander is larger and has a poorly defined dorsal stripe that

Adult
*Skamania County,
Washington*

WILLIAM LEONARD

Adult
*Skamania County,
Washington*

WILLIAM LEONARD

Adult
*King County,
Washington*

CHARLES M. CRISAFULLI

Adult
*Skamania County,
Washington*

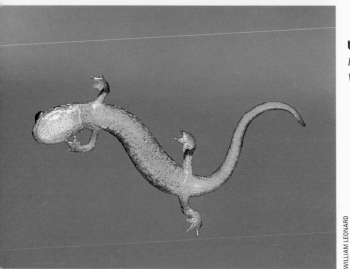

Underside of an adult
*Kittitas County,
Washington*

Underside of an adult
*King County,
Washington*

does not extend to tip of tail, a longer outer hind toe and a lateral surface with large flecks of dorsal stripe color. The Oregon Slender Salamander has four toes on all feet, a black venter and lateral surface with large, white flecking. The Long-toed Salamander has longer toes and lacks a nasolabial groove.

Distribution: The Larch Mountain Salamander is endemic to Washington and Oregon, where it has a restricted range. Populations are found along a 58 km section of the Columbia River Gorge (both north and south of the Columbia River). Larch Mountain Salamanders also are patchily distributed to the north in the Washington Cascade Range and to the south in the Oregon Cascade Range. The north-south range extends about 200 km. In Washington, Larch Mountain Salamanders occur in Clark, Cowlitz, Skamania, Lewis, King, Klickitat and Kittitas Counties. In Oregon, they are found in Multnomah and Hood River Counties. As of March 2003, there were 138 known Larch Mountain Salamander sites; 112 of these were in Washington.

Life History: Little is known about Larch Mountain Salamander reproduction. Courtship has not been described. Males attain sexual maturity at 3–3.5 years. Females are sexually mature at 4 years of age and probably produce a clutch once every 2 years. Individuals captured as adults have lived 8 years in captivity, suggesting longevity may exceed 12 years.

Natural History: Larch Mountain Salamander surface activity is tightly coupled with cool, wet weather conditions that occur during spring and autumn. Surface activity also may be limited to a few weeks each year in some portion of the species' range. These salamanders are largely nocturnal, but during wet conditions they may be active during the day. Their diet includes small, ground-dwelling arthropods such as mites, springtails, spiders and beetles. In turn, Larch Mountain Salamanders likely are preyed upon by snakes, shrews and large, predatory insects. Larch Mountain Salamanders occur with Western Red-backed, Dunn's, Oregon Slender, Van Dyke's, Ensatina, Cascade Torrent and Long-toed Salamanders, and Coastal Tailed Frogs.

Habitat: Larch Mountain Salamanders occur in a wide array of terrestrial habitats, ranging from 50–1250 m elevation. Strong environmental gradients (temperature and moisture), coupled with varying geologic history and disturbance regimes (volcanoes and wildfire), have created a complex mosaic of habitat patches across the species' range. Within this landscape mosaic, the species occurs in old-growth forest; young, naturally regenerated forests with residual late-successional features (large logs, bark piles); shrub-dominated communities; scree; talus; and lava-tube entrances where debris has accumulated. The surface geology and soil formation in the central portion of the species' range have been influenced dramatically by pumice deposits from volcanic eruptions. In this "pumice zone," the species appears to be tightly associated with old-growth forest and is often found beneath woody debris (bark, branches, slabs). In the remainder of the species' range, where surface rock is abundant, populations are found in numerous vegetation types, and animals are generally found under gravel and cobbles, and under woody debris to a lesser extent.

Remarks: The Larch Mountain Salamander is a rare endemic species that is patchily distributed throughout its range. Low dispersal, low fecundity, patchy distribution and narrow physiological tolerance limits have likely led to the relatively high genetic variation among populations. Larch Mountain Salamanders are on the Washington and Oregon State and U.S. Forest Service Sensitive Species lists.

SISKIYOU MOUNTAINS SALAMANDER

Plethodon stormi   HIGHTON AND BRAME

Authors: David Clayton and Richard S. Nauman

Description: The Siskiyou Mountains Salamander is a **slim, long-bodied woodland salamander.** Adults measure 45–70 mm SVL and 70–132 mm TL. An adult *Plethodon stormi* has a modal **number of 17 costal grooves and 4–5.5 intercostal folds between adpressed limbs.** Adults are chocolate brown to purplish brown and usually possess varying amounts of white to yellowish flecking on the head, sides, dorsum and limbs. Juveniles are usually at least 20 mm SVL and 40 mm TL and tend to be black or very dark brown with flecking. Juveniles also often exhibit a light brown or tan dorsal stripe and are gray ventrally.

Variation: The number of costal grooves differs between the Klamath

Basin populations and the Applegate populations. In addition, emerging genetic results have found distinct lineages that suggest a complex evolutionary history.

Eggs: While no nests of this species have yet been found, it is likely that they are similar to those of other western plethodontids. Eggs in gravid females typically measure 4–5 mm in diameter, and clutch size varies from 8–10 eggs. There is no free-living larval stage; hatchlings emerge as juvenile salamanders.

Similar Species: The Del Norte Salamander has a somewhat longer body, 6.5–7.5 intercostal folds between adpressed limbs, and a reddish or copper stripe in juveniles. The Scott Bar Salamander has 2–3 intercostal folds between adpressed limbs. The Black Salamander has a black ground color with a profuse green to bronze wash along the sides of the animal. The Clouded Salamander has a dorsal ground color of brown with brassy patches and squared-off toe tips. Ensatina has a shorter body and a distinct constriction at the base of the tail, and adpressed limbs overlap. Juvenile Ensatinas and Black Salamanders also have yellow upper arms. However, the juveniles of all these species may sometimes be difficult to distinguish in the field.

Distribution: The Siskiyou Mountains Salamander is found only in a 136,595 ha area of northwestern California and southwestern Oregon. It occurs primarily in northern Siskiyou County, California, southern Jackson County, Oregon, and extreme southeast Josephine County, Oregon. To date, there are approximately 200 localities known for the species. In Oregon, Siskiyou Mountains Salamanders are known to occur within approximately 1 km of the eastern edge of the Del Norte Salamander's range. In California, there may be an area of contact between these two salamander species within the Klamath

Adult

Applegate River, Siskiyou County, California

Adult

Seiad Valley, Siskiyou County, California

Adult
*Applegate River,
Siskiyou County,
California*

WILLIAM LEONARD

Adult
*Applegate River,
Siskiyou County,
California*

WILLIAM LEONARD

Juvenile
*Applegate River,
Siskiyou County,
California*

WILLIAM LEONARD

River Valley west of Seiad Valley, California. In both Oregon and California, this species has been found at elevations ranging from 488–1830 m.

Life History: Females likely lay eggs every other year during the spring within underground chambers where they may brood them until the eggs hatch in the fall. Juvenile Siskiyou Mountains Salamanders apparently do hatch in the fall. Reproductive maturity likely occurs about the fourth or fifth year, and longevity may be as much as 12–15 years.

Natural History: Siskiyou Mountains Salamanders are active near the surface during warm and wet periods, usually during the spring when it no longer freezes during the night or in the fall after at least 1 inch of rain falls. They feed primarily on invertebrates such as ants, mites, spiders, springtails, millipedes and beetles. Ants are the primary food in the spring, while mites, beetles and millipedes constitute the primary prey in the fall. Little is known about potential predators, but extensive scarring and tail loss on some individuals suggest that rodents or shrews may prey on this species. There are some snakes, such as Ring-necked Snakes, that co-occur with Siskiyou Mountains Salamanders and that also may be predators on this species.

Habitat: This species is considered to be a talus or forested rocky habitat obligate. While Siskiyou Mountains Salamanders can be found in various forested situations with rocky substrates, they are most closely associated with older or late-successional forests with closed canopies.

Remarks: Natural disturbance events such as catastrophic fire, as well as many land management activities such as timber harvest, road building and rock quarrying have the potential to impact this species. The legal status of this species varies by state and federal agency, and it is listed as Threatened in California, a Sensitive Species in Oregon, a Sensitive Species for the U.S. Forest Service, and a Species of Concern for the Bureau of Land Management. The U.S. Fish and Wildlife Service was recently petitioned to list the Siskiyou Mountains Salamander under the Endangered Species Act. Several federal agencies are currently developing a range-wide conservation plan for this species. Populations of *Plethodon* found south of the Klamath River in the vicinity of Seiad Valley and Scott Bar, California, represent a previously undescribed species, the Scott Bar Salamander *(Plethodon asupak)*.

VAN DYKE'S SALAMANDER

Plethodon vandykei　　　VAN DENBURGH

Authors: Lawrence L.C. Jones
and Charles M. Crisafulli

Description: This is a relatively **stocky and long-limbed woodland salamander, having an average of 14 costal grooves and ½–3 intercostal folds between adpressed limbs.** Van Dyke's Salamander has slightly webbed toes and a relatively short tail. It possesses **parotoid glands,** which are somewhat inconspicuous, resembling head musculature. Adults have a yellowish to reddish dorsal stripe, which may or may not be distinct from the color on the sides and venter. **It usually appears that the dorsal stripe has "drips" of color extending from the dorsal stripe onto the sides;** this is most conspicuous on juveniles or dark-phase adults. The dorsal stripe is brighter on the tail than on the body. There is a triangle of lighter dorsal color between the eyes

and snout. Dark-phase adults have a yellow throat and white-speckled venter. Adults reach about 60 mm SVL and 110 mm TL. Proportionally, juveniles have a larger head, shorter tail and a more pronounced dorsal stripe compared to adults. The venter and sides of those destined to be light-phase adults will lose dark pigments as they mature. Thus, **juveniles of both light and dark phases have the characteristic yellow throat and white-speckled venter, with a bold dorsal stripe, usually displaying the distinctive "drips."**

Variation: Three color phases are mentioned in the literature: dark, yellow and rose. However, it is often difficult to differentiate the yellow and rose phases, and these are here collectively termed "light phase." Light-phase animals lose dark pigments as they mature, whereas the dark-phase animals do not. Yellow-phase individuals are usually more of a yellow-green to ochre color than yellow per se, and rose-phase animals are usually salmon (light orange-red) in color, with intensities varying geographically. Light-phase animals are found throughout the range, but dark-phase animals are found only in the Cascade Range. At most high-elevation sites in the Cascade Range, light-phase animals comprise < 10% of the population, but some populations (especially at lower elevation sites) may be composed of primarily light-phase individuals.

Eggs: Seven nests have been found, all on the Olympic Peninsula. All but one were found inside the upper surface of large, decomposing conifer logs near streams; one was under a rock. There is no free-living larval stage; hatchlings emerge as juvenile salamanders.

Similar Species: Light-phase adults superficially resemble Ensatina but have 14 rather than 12 costal grooves and lack the constricted tail base. Dunn's and Western Red-backed Salamanders have

Yellow-phase adult
Pacific County,
Washington

WILLIAM LEONARD

Juvenile
Pacific County,
Washington

WILLIAM LEONARD

Dark-phase adult
Lewis County,
Washington

WILLIAM LEONARD

Adult attending egg mass in log
Clallam County, Washington

Dark-phase adult
Lewis County, Washington

Adult
Thurston County, Washington

more costal grooves and shorter limbs and lack parotoid glands. Larch Mountain Salamanders lack parotoid glands and usually have a scalloped dorsal stripe, a pinkish venter and a single phalanx on the outer hind toe. Dark-phase adults and juveniles of both phases resemble the Long-toed Salamander, but the former have a nasolabial groove and shorter toes. Coeur d'Alene Salamanders are very similar to dark-phase adults, but the ranges of the two species are not known to overlap.

Distribution: This species is endemic to Washington State, occurring in three disjunct populations: Willapa Hills (Pacific, Wahkiakum and western Lewis Counties); the west slope of the Cascade Range from the vicinity of Canyon Creek to the north side of Mount Rainier; and west and south portions of the Olympic Peninsula (apparently absent from rain-shadow sides).

Life History: Presumably, Van Dyke's has a courtship display like other wood-land salamanders. All known nests were laid in May, but Van Dyke's may have a prolonged breeding season in some areas. Females attend the eggs, which are usually suspended from the top of a nest chamber. Nest sites remain moist, even during the summer, and the temperature inside the chamber is moderated from outside extremes, thus providing ideal conditions for egg development. Van Dyke's probably breeds every two years. Animals are known to live at least 12 years.

Natural History: Van Dyke's Salamanders are most active in the spring and fall and are most likely to be encountered during relatively warm rainy periods. Presumably, they feed on small invertebrates. In the Cascade Range, they are commonly found associated with Cascade Torrent Salamanders and Coastal Tailed Frogs, and occasionally with Larch Mountain, Western Red-backed and Coastal Giant Salamanders. In the Olympics, they are commonly found with Olympic Torrent Salamanders and Western Red-backed Salamanders. In the Willapa Hills, they may be found with Western Red-backed Salamanders, Dunn's Salamanders and Columbia Torrent Salamanders. In coastal areas, they are usually less abundant than other species, even in favorable habitat.

Habitat: This species seems to have some habitat differences, depending on geography, but throughout their range, Van Dyke's Salamanders are often associated with rocky, steep-walled stream valleys. In the Olympics, they are most common in old-growth forests, where colluvial rock and large fallen logs are abundant. In the Willapa Hills, they are commonly found in both woody and rocky substrates. A favored microhabitat seems to be between slabs of wood or bark on large logs near streams. In the Cascade Range, they are usually found under cobble and sometimes wood, within a few meters of a stream. They are found most often in exfoliating rock, valley wall seeps with exfoliating rock or gravel, splash zones at the base of waterfalls, or adjacent to chutes and cascades. Van Dyke's Salamanders survived and persisted for 25 years at numerous locations severely disturbed by the 1980 eruption of Mount St. Helens.

Remarks: Van Dyke's Salamanders warrant genetic study because of the variation in color patterns and presumed differences in habitat use among sub-populations across its range. This is an uncommon salamander with a spotty distribution, but animals may be locally abundant. Because of its relative rarity and specialized habitat, this is a Species of Concern to state and federal agencies in Washington.

WESTERN RED-BACKED SALAMANDER

Plethodon vehiculum   COOPER

Authors: Kristiina Ovaska and Theodore M. Davis

Description: The Western Red-backed Sal-amander is a small, terrestrial salamander. Adults measure about 40–58 mm SVL and 115 mm TL. The body is slender, the legs short. **Costal grooves typically number 16** but can vary from 14–18. **A broad, mid-dorsal stripe extends to the tip of the tail and usually has even, well-defined edges.** The color of the stripe varies from reddish orange (most common) to olive green, tan or yellow. Small, dark flecks are usually present on the head and stripe. The background color is dark gray or brown. The gray venter is sprinkled with white flecking. Adult males can be distinguished from females by the presence of premaxillary teeth that protrude through the upper lip, a square-shaped jaw (rounded in females),

and a small, swollen fold or lobe on each side of the vent (the vent of females is slightly concave, with pleated margins). Newly hatched young are very slender and about 15 mm SVL. The juvenile's dorsal stripe is often brighter than that of adults.

Variation: Melanistic individuals with varying degrees of dark pigmentation on the dorsum, including all-black, unstriped individuals, are common at some localities. Erythric individuals (with the reddish stripe-color invading the sides) and other unusual color morphs, such as partial albinos, piebald and amelanistic, are encountered occasionally.

Eggs: The grape-like egg cluster is attached to the nesting hollow by a broad, gelatinous base. Individual eggs are yellowish cream in color, about 4.3–5.0 mm in diameter, and enclosed in 2 transparent envelopes. Clutch size is 7–11 eggs, based on a small number of field observations. The number of ovarian eggs in dissected specimens (reported range: 5–19 eggs) shows a positive correlation with the body size of the female. There is no free-living larval stage; hatchlings emerge as juvenile salamanders.

Similar Species: The Long-toed Salamander also has a broad dorsal stripe but lacks the nasolabial groove and has a keeled, rather than rounded, tail. The larger Dunn's Salamander has a greenish or tan dorsal stripe with ragged edges, and the stripe does not extend to the tail tip; flecks that are the color of the stripe occur on the sides. Other sympatric, striped species of *Plethodon* that might be confusing are the Larch Mountain Salamander, which can be distinguished by its red-orange venter; the Del Norte Salamander, which is more elon-gate and has a longer tail and shorter legs; and the Van Dyke's Salamander, which is more robust and has slightly webbed toes and parotoid glands. Small juveniles may be difficult to distinguish from other

Red-striped morph
Jefferson County, Washington

Melanistic morph
Thurston County, Washington

Yellow-striped morph
Jefferson County, Washington

Partially amelanistic morph
Jefferson County, Washington

sympatric *Plethodon*. Unusually patterned Western Red-backed Salamanders are often confused with other species.

Distribution: The species' distribution extends from southwestern British Columbia through western Washington to southwestern Oregon. In British Columbia, it is found throughout Vancouver Island but seems to be limited to elevations < 500 m; on the mainland, it occurs west to Hope and north to near Pemberton. In Washington, it ranges from the coast to the western Cascade Range, where it is found up to elevations of about 760 m. It occurs on some smaller islands off the west coast of Vancouver Island and Washington but is notably absent from the Gulf Islands in the Georgia Strait. The species' range extends east to about Stevenson, Skamania County, Washington, in the Columbia Gorge, and south to near Canyonville, Douglas County. The species is absent from most of the northern portion of the Oregon Cascade Range. In the southern Cascade Range, a distribution record exists from 1370 m.

Life History: Like other western plethodontids, this species is completely terrestrial and has direct development. Eggs are laid in moist, secluded locations on land sometime in spring and hatch in early fall into miniature versions of adults. Female parental care of eggs probably occurs but is poorly documented. Males mature at about 38–43 mm SVL and females at about 42–44 mm SVL. Sexual maturity is reached in 2–3 years, and thereafter females reproduce every second year or less frequently. Courtship occurs from fall to early winter. Mate choice and courtship involve chemical cues. As in other plethodontids, fertilization is internal but indirect and involves the transfer of a package of sperm (spermatophore) from the male to the female. The female stores the sperm, which is then used to fertilize

her eggs the following spring. Individuals can live more than 10 years, but few reach this age in the wild.

Natural History: Peak periods of surface activity occur during moist conditions in the spring and fall, but individuals can be found above ground any time of the year during suitable conditions. These salamanders are primarily nocturnal and can be found exposed on the forest floor on calm, wet nights. The diet consists of a wide variety of invertebrates. Unlike several other species of *Plethodon*, individuals do not defend foraging territories, but males fight and show aggression toward each other during the mating period. Known predators include the Common Gartersnake and the Shrew-mole. Various birds, small mammals and other snakes probably also prey on these salamanders, and ground beetles may take small young.

Habitat: This species inhabits moist coniferous and mixed forests. It can be found in all forest ages, but abundance is much reduced in recently logged areas. Microhabitats include spaces within and under decaying wood, rocks and vegetation. Crevices within stable, moist talus provide especially good habitat. During wet conditions, these salamanders can be found within the forest floor litter away from cover-objects. Egg-laying sites include cavities under rocks in talus and under bark on the ground.

Remarks: Western Red-backed Salamanders show a high degree of site-tenacity and typically confine their activities to areas of only a few meters in diameter. The abundance of these salamanders varies widely among sites and can reach extraordinarily high densities in suitable habitats; average surface densities up to 3.7 salamanders/m^2 have been reported on Vancouver Island.

Notes:

Diagrams:

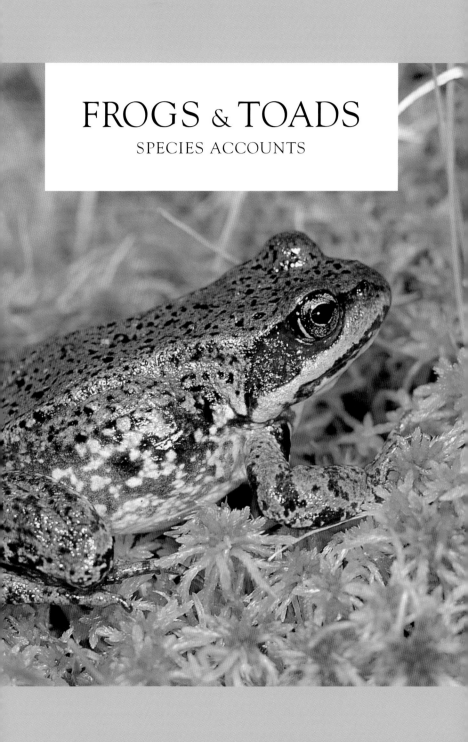

FROGS & TOADS
SPECIES ACCOUNTS

ROCKY MOUNTAIN TAILED FROG

Ascaphus montanus   MITTLEMAN AND MYERS

Authors: Evelyn L. Bull and Matthew Snook

Description: The Rocky Mountain Tailed Frog can be brown, reddish brown, khaki green, greenish yellow, or gray with yellow and gray mottling. The **eye has a vertical pupil,** and the tympanum is absent. **Males have a prominent, cloacal "tail"** (lacking in females) used for copulation. The **outer hind toes of both sexes are broad and flattened.** Females measure to 51 mm TL and males (tail excluded) to 45 mm TL.

Eggs and Larvae: A small clutch (45–60) of pea-sized, white eggs is deposited in a gelatinous string under a large rock in a stream. The eggs of tailed frogs are the largest (about 4–5 mm), have the narrowest range of thermal tolerance (5–18.5°C) and have the slowest embryonic developmental rate of any North American frog. Tadpoles

are black or brown and often have a whitish spot on the tip of the tail. The tadpoles are unique in possessing an oral disk with a modified, sucker-like device that enables them to attach to rocks in a swift current. Populations in the Rocky Mountains exhibit a 3-year larval period. Age classes of tadpoles can be separated by total length and extent of limb emergence. Tadpoles that have just hatched are cream-colored and 10–12 mm in length. Later, the tadpoles reach up to 75 mm in length and may have emergent legs during much of the third year.

Similar Species: The tailed frog taxon has recently been divided into two species, based on genetic and morphological data: the Rocky Mountain Tailed Frog and the Coastal (formerly Olympic) Tailed Frog. The two species are most easily distinguished by distribution. Pacific Treefrogs have sticky, round pads on the tips of the toes. True frogs (*Rana* spp.) and true toads (*Bufo* spp.) do not have flattened, outer hind toes. No other tadpole in its range has a round, sucker-like mouth.

Distribution: Rocky Mountain Tailed Frogs occur from extreme southeastern British Columbia south through western Montana to extreme southeastern Washington, northeastern Oregon and south-central Idaho. Southern populations are above 975 m. Two small population groups in British Columbia are geographically isolated by the Rocky Mountain Trench, which extends north of Flathead Lake, Montana.

Life History: Mating occurs in early fall. Secondary sexual characteristics of the male (black nuptial tubercles of the palm, forearm, ventral surface of shoulders, and chin) are highly developed during the breeding season. Tailed frogs are unique in that they copulate rather than spawn; fertilization is internal, and sperm are retained by the female. Egg-laying occurs nearly a year

Adult male
*Shoshone County,
Idaho*

Adult female
*Shoshone County,
Idaho*

Adult male
*Benewah County,
Idaho*

Adult male
*Shoshone County,
Idaho*

BRAD MOON

Eggs
*Ravalli County,
Montana*

DAVID PILLIOD

Tadpole
*Ravalli County,
Montana*

DAVID PILLIOD

after mating, from June until early August. Egg-laying occurs in July in Idaho, northeastern Oregon and southeastern Washington, coincident with the end of spring runoff in some areas. Eggs hatch in August and September. Larvae transform in 3 years, usually by September. Males become sexually mature at 7 years and females at 8 years in Montana. The females have a biennial reproductive cycle. The eggs are visible through the ventral abdominal wall during two summers before egg-laying. Rocky Mountain Tailed Frogs may live in excess of 14 years.

Natural History: Rocky Mountain Tailed Frogs are similar to other tailed frogs in that they inhabit headwater streams in isolated, discrete populations and show limited movements. Adults are primarily nocturnal, although they are sometimes active during daylight hours. Level of activity is related to both air temperature and humidity, with tailed frogs preferring low temperatures and high humidity. Adults move away from the stream to forage on invertebrates, then return to the stream before dawn and find cover under rocks. In drier environments, foraging movements may be limited to the immediate riparian areas. Adults are extremely philopatric (showing no directional movement) in most areas, but they may move downstream in summer as streams dry. Larvae feed on diatoms. Predators of tailed frogs include Brook, Rainbow, Cutthroat and Bull Trout, gartersnakes, Mink, Raccoon, River Otter and Belted Kingfisher.

Habitat: Adults and tadpoles inhabit cold, swift, permanently flowing mountain streams. Within a watershed, distribution is largely restricted to the headwaters or areas of cold water (7 to 18°C summer temperatures) and coarse substrate. Geology is therefore a primary factor governing tailed frog distribution, as it influences the substrate and sedimentation in streams.

Coarse substances provide larger and more stable interstitial spaces in which tadpoles can forage and seek refuge from channel disturbance events and predators. Stable streams typically have a coarse, anchored substrate and provide the best habitat. Low-gradient streams have a higher quantity of fine sediments and are vulnerable to high water temperatures and algal blooms in late summer, providing poorer habitat. Steep drainages are frequently susceptible to hazardous debris flows, rapid runoff and extreme peak discharges. Tadpole density is highest in streams dominated by cobble. Tadpoles and adults overwinter under rocks in streams.

Remarks: This species is moderately widespread and locally common in the Rocky Mountain region, although population trends are unknown. Tailed frogs are rare in drainages that have been completely logged. The removal of coarse, woody debris in streams occupied by this species increases the erosion of stream banks and the release of fine sediments. Small headwater streams and creeks with unstable beds are the most vulnerable to this type of impact. Rocky Mountain Tailed Frogs cannot tolerate high temperatures or high rates of evaporative water loss that may result from a loss of canopy incurred in harvesting. Conservation measures include protecting headwater stream habitat, leaving structures that reduce sediment input, reducing wind-throw near streams, and providing for a long-term source of downed wood.

COASTAL TAILED FROG

Ascaphus truei   STEJNEGER

Author: Herbert A. Brown

Description: The dorsum of adults is brown, reddish brown or gray, with yellow and gray mottling. The underside of the body is light gray. **The eye has a vertical pupil,** and there is usually a dark eye stripe. There is no tympanum. **Males have a prominent, cloacal "tail" (lacking in females), and the outer hind toes of both sexes are broad and flattened.** Females measure to 51 mm long and males (tail excluded) to 43 mm.

   Variation: Some tadpoles are variegated (with black, brown and yellow-gold), others are granitic (black and speckled with white spots). They may color-match the stream substrate. Albino tadpoles have been found at two creeks, but they are rare.

   Eggs and Larvae: The eggs are large (5 mm diameter) and entirely white. They are deposited in two long, pearl-like strings,

enclosed by a transparent jelly covering and attached to the underside of large rocks in streams. Clutch size is about 60 eggs, but several females may share a communal site as an "egg nest" composed of 150 eggs. Tadpoles are adapted to stream life. They have a large, sucker-like mouth (oral disc) and a streamlined body and tail. Tadpole color is usually black or dark brown, with a conspicuous white spot on the tip of the long tail. Tadpoles grow to about 50 mm.

   Similar Species: Recently, the Rocky Mountain Tailed Frog (*Ascaphus montanus*) was described as a separate species, based on genetics. The coastal form now is called the Coastal Tailed Frog, and the previous name (Olympic Tailed Frog) no longer applies. The range of the Coastal Tailed Frog does not overlap that of the Rocky Mountain Tailed Frog. Pacific Treefrogs have sticky, round pads on the tips of the toes. True frogs (*Rana* spp.) and true toads (*Bufo* spp.) do not have flattened, outer hind toes. No other tadpole in its range has a large, round, sucker-like mouth.

   Distribution: The Coastal Tailed Frog occurs throughout the Cascades, Olympics and the Coast Ranges from southwestern British Columbia through western Washington and Oregon into northwestern California. Coastal Tailed Frogs are known to occur from sea level to 1600 m in Mount Rainier National Park.

   Life History: Mating takes place in late summer and early fall, and the female stores sperm until the following June or early July. Females living at high elevations probably lay eggs in alternate years. The testes of male tailed frogs are especially large and have a high sperm concentration; this may be an advantage when females (as many as 20) hibernate at communal sites in the stream, and a single male may discover (perhaps by smell?) and inseminate each female in this aggregation. During early summer, females deposit a gelatinous string of eggs

Adult male crawling on a stream bottom
Kittitas County, Washington

WILLIAM LEONARD

Female underwater in a stream
Kittitas County, Washington

WILLIAM LEONARD

Adult male
Linn County, Oregon

WILLIAM LEONARD

A pair in amplexus
*Multnomah County,
Oregon*

**Strings of eggs on the
underside of a rock**
British Columbia

**Underside of a
tadpole adhering
to glass container**
*Snohomish County,
Washington*

onto the underside of large rocks in the stream. Embryos are cold-adapted, and they develop slowly, with hatchlings appearing in late summer or fall. The hatching tadpoles have a large supply of yolk still present in the mid-gut. The duration of the tadpole period and body size at metamorphosis are variable. Most amphibian species living in montane habitats where temperature is low have a long larval period and large body size at metamorphosis, while populations at low elevations have shorter larval periods and smaller size at metamorphosis. In the Coastal Tailed Frog, the duration of the larval period may be 1, 2, 3 or 4 years. At high elevations, it may take an additional 5 or 6 years for froglets to reach maturity. The time required for growth and development of embryos and tadpoles is the longest of any known amphibian.

Natural History: Coastal Tailed Frogs are most often observed during the summer months when water levels are low. Adults are most active at night, but they are very secretive and seldom observed. At night, the frogs emerge and feed upon insects at the stream edge. During rainy periods, these frogs may be found in nearby forests. Tadpole mouthparts provide suction for attachment to rocks in swift-flowing streams, and the complex tooth rows scrape diatoms (one-celled algae) from rock surfaces. Coastal Tailed Frog tadpoles can be the dominant herbivore in small, headwater streams, and they may constitute 90% of the herbivore biomass. The sparse food resources of these streams may control the growth rate and abundance of tadpoles.

Habitat: Coastal Tailed Frogs are often found in cold, rocky, mountain streams in western forests. Tadpoles can be found by turning over rocks in streams. Juveniles and adults occur along stream banks and in the near-stream riparian corridor, on the forest floor and in vegetation. They can disperse overland and have been observed upslope and on ridgeline roads.

Remarks: Tailed frogs belong to the most primitive of frog families; their nearest relatives live in New Zealand. As an adaptation to stream life, the lungs of this frog are greatly reduced (decreasing buoyancy), and breathing takes place across the surface of the skin. In addition, the fingertips are hardened like claws and assist the frog to crawl and dig among rocks along the stream bottom. Also, the body is somewhat flattened, which may assist in directing the frog downward in the swift currents of the stream. Neither the female nor the male can produce any vocalization, and both the external ear and the middle ear bone are absent. The loss of these structures is likely an adaptation to a "noisy," rocky stream habitat, where sounds are not important to the daily life of these frogs. The way that Coastal Tailed Frogs move is unusual. Typical frogs generally hop on land and use strong, simultaneous (symmetric) motions of the hind legs to swim in water. In contrast, tailed frogs jump on land and swim by using alternate (asymmetric) movements of the hind legs, and this is considered to be a primitive trait. Tailed frog populations may be severely reduced or eliminated by extensive timber harvest and road building, which contribute to sedimentation of streams and increased stream temperatures.

GREAT BASIN SPADEFOOT

Spea intermontana   COPE

Author: Lisa A. Hallock

Description: The Great Basin Spadefoot is a small to medium-sized, light-colored toad with a plump body, short limbs and a blunt, upturned snout. Adults are 40–63 mm SVL. The hallmark of the genus is **a single, sharp-edged, black "spade" on the inner edge of each hind foot,** used for burrowing. The skin is moist, soft and rather smooth. The overall color is light gray, olive or brown, with two light streaks running down the back. There are also small, raised, dark blotches, typically with red or orange centers, scattered over the dorsal surface. The underside is whitish. Males are sexually mature at 40 mm SVL, females around 45 mm SVL. Mature males have a dusky throat and, during the breeding season, have dark nuptial pads on the innermost front toes.

Eggs and Larvae: Eggs are laid in small, loose clusters of 10–40 eggs. The mass is approximately 15–20 mm, irregular in shape, and the outline of individual eggs is distinct, somewhat like a cluster of grapes. Individual eggs are small, with the diameter of the ovum and jelly together measuring less than 5 mm. The eggs are easily detached from the mass. The masses are attached to vegetation or laid directly on the substrate. Tadpoles have a slightly flattened body shape with closely set, raised, dorsal eyes. They have prominent nostrils and a tail fin that terminates at the tail-body junction. The coloration is dark with metallic markings on the dorsal body and golden iridescence on the abdomen. The tail musculature is light in color, and the tail fins are finely reticulated with light brown. The dorsal fin narrows toward the tip and ends just past the termination of the tail musculature. When viewed from above, the triangular-shaped head is distinct from the abdomen, although the outer silhouette of the body is continuous. Tadpoles grow to between 30–70 mm TL before metamorphosis. Newly transformed spadefoot toads range in size from approximately 10–20 mm SVL.

Similar Species: True toads (*Bufo* spp.) have well-developed parotoid glands, two light-colored tubercles on the underside of the feet, and horizontally oval pupils. Other species' eggs may be distinguished by size and shape. Individual eggs of the Long-toed Salamander are larger, with a total diameter, including jelly layers, that is usually greater than 10 mm. Pacific Treefrog egg masses are more rounded in general appearance (not like a bunch of grapes), with individual eggs that are tightly connected to one another.

Distribution: The Great Basin Spadefoot inhabits the western United States and British Columbia from south-central British Columbia to the Colorado River, and from east of the Cascade Range and Sierra

Adult
*Harney County,
Oregon*

WILLIAM LEONARD

**Juvenile burrowing
into loose sand**
*Grant County,
Washington*

WILLIAM LEONARD

**Close-up of the
"spade" on hind foot**
*Benton County,
Washington*

WILLIAM LEONARD

Adult
*Benton County,
Washington*

Egg mass
*Grant County,
Washington*

Tadpole
*Okanogan County,
Washington*

Nevada to west of the Rocky Mountain divide. In the region of this book, it occurs in the Thompson, Similkameen and Okanogan Valleys and Grand Forks area of British Columbia, south into the Columbia Basin of Washington and the Great Basin of eastern Oregon, and east into the Snake River drainage of Idaho.

Life History: In general, the breeding season is prolonged, starting in late March and extending into June. Duration at each site depends on site conditions such as temperature, pool duration and food availability. Eggs hatch in 2–3 days, or longer under cooler conditions. Larval development, on average, takes between 1–2 months. Newly metamorphosed spadefoots have been observed to disperse from natal ponds en masse. They mature in 2–3 years and may live up to about 10 years.

Natural History: Great Basin Spadefoots are terrestrial and nocturnal after metamorphosis. They are adapted to arid habitats, where they survive dry and cold periods by burrowing underground and remaining dormant for long periods. The advertisement call during breeding is a series of repeated, monotonous, grating, snore-like "w-a-a-h" or "kw-a-a-h" calls, each lasting about 0.5–1 second. The calls can be heard over a distance of 200 m. Tadpoles consume a variety of organic matter, including algae, plant material and carrion. Under some conditions, tadpoles are cannibalistic on eggs, hatchlings and smaller tadpoles. Adults eat a variety of insects. Spadefoots have irritating, distasteful skin secretions that may help protect them from some predators. Predators on adults include Coyotes and Burrowing Owls. Crows and gartersnakes have been observed consuming tadpoles.

Habitat: Terrestrial habitats are mainly shrub-steppe, grassland and open Ponderosa Pine forest. In the Columbia Basin, spadefoots persist in some areas that have been converted to irrigated agricultural land. Breeding takes place in a variety of permanent and temporary waters, including rain-filled pools, springs, sloughs, irrigation ditches, still-water edges of streams, and ponds.

Remarks: There is some debate about whether the western spadefoots, including the Great Basin Spadefoot, should be kept in the genus *Scaphiopus* rather than *Spea*. At this time, most authors appear to have accepted *Spea*. The skin-gland secretions of spadefoots are irritating to mucous membranes and will cause burning and irritation of the eyes and nose. Handling spadefoots causes some people to sneeze.

WESTERN TOAD

Bufo boreas　　　　　　BAIRD AND GIRARD

Author: Deanna H. Olson

Description: This "true toad" has **dry, warty skin, pronounced oval parotoid glands** behind the eyes, and **a stocky body form.** Adults may be 55–145 mm SVL, with females growing larger than males. Metamorphic toadlets are 6–13 mm SVL. Dorsal color is variable (green, tan, reddish brown to brown, or gray to black), and toads can be mottled or have more solid coloring. Dorsal gland (wart) color may differ from the background color and can be brown, rust, red, or yellow and ringed by black. A **light, mid-dorsal stripe,** a key characteristic of these toads, can be white, buff or light green. Ventral color is white or cream to a light yellow or yellow-green, with gray to black specks. The ventral-groin area may be gray. Metamorphs are more uniformly brown in color, may lack a

dorsal stripe and may have strikingly bright yellow or orange tubercles on the undersides of their feet.

Variation: Adult sizes vary with locality. Toads in populations at higher elevations or in areas with shorter growing seasons may be substantially smaller. Color is variable, and the mid-dorsal stripe may not be present. Skin can vary from smooth to warty. Four genetic lineages have been identified: northwest, southwest, southern Utah and southern Rocky Mountains. Currently recognized subspecies include the Boreal Toad, *B. boreas boreas,* the form occurring in the Northwest and throughout most of the species' range; and the California Toad, *B. b. halophilus,* found in California south of about Chico in the Central Valley, but extending to both the coast and Nevada. The California Toad has less dark mottling, wider head, larger eyes and smaller feet. Some sources include the Amargosa Toad as a third subspecies *(B. b. nelsoni),* which occurs only in the Oasis Valley along the Amargosa River, Nye County, Nevada. Amargosa Toads have narrower heads, longer snouts and shorter limbs.

Eggs and Larvae: Jet-black eggs are oviposited in dual strings which may appear to zigzag. Clutch size varies with female body size, from a few thousand to > 17,000 eggs. Egg strings occur as single clutches or in multiple, overlapping masses. Tadpoles are black in appearance. The tail fin trunk is black, and the fin has pigmentation, with the dorsal tail fin darker than the ventral portion. The abdomen has a fine golden shimmer in bright light. Rarely, individuals will have gold pigment that is more extensive, forming small blotches on the body and tail musculature.

Similar Species: Woodhouse's Toads *(Bufo woodhousii)* have a prominent cranial crest behind each eye and more elongated parotoid glands. The

Portrait of an adult

*Shoshone County,
Idaho*

Adult

*Okanogan County,
Washington*

**Pairs in amplexus
with strings of eggs**

*Grant County,
Oregon*

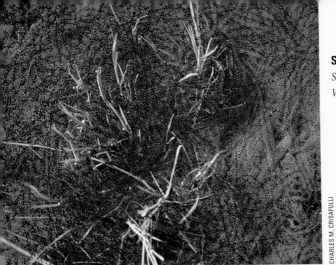

Strings of eggs
Skamania County, Washington

CHARLES M. CRISAFULLI

Tadpole
Thurston County, Washington

WILLIAM LEONARD

Juvenile
Thurston County, Washington

WILLIAM LEONARD

characteristic *Bufo* horizontal oval pupils and mid-dorsal stripe distinguish Western Toads from Great Basin Spadefoots, which have vertically elliptical pupils. Tailed frogs have vertical pupils, no external ear and broad, flattened, outer hind toes. The Foothill Yellow-legged Frog has a fine-grained, warty appearance, smooth ventral skin, inconspicuous ear and no parotoid glands. Other ranid frogs have dorsolateral folds and smoother skin. Treefrogs have smooth skin, a dark mask and toe pads. The black Western Toad tadpoles are easily distinguished from sympatric *Rana* and *Pseudacris,* which are golden to dark brown, with silver to gold flecking on their sides or ventral surface. Western Toad eggs are in strings, in contrast to the round clutches or single ova produced by other amphibians.

Distribution: Western Toads occur from Baja California throughout the western U.S. (California, Nevada, Oregon, Washington, Idaho and Utah), British Columbia to Alaska, and barely into the Yukon Territory. They range eastward to southwestern Alberta, western Montana, western and southern Wyoming, Colorado and north-central New Mexico. Several notable gaps in distribution occur throughout the range. Western Toads can be found from sea level to > 3600 m elevation.

Life History: Western Toads are active from about January through October and breed from January to July. Mating pairs in amplexus often oviposit eggs synchronously and communally, with hundreds of thousands to millions of eggs being deposited at larger aggregations. Hatching occurs within 3–12 days. Tadpoles school, and large schools may extend along lake shorelines. Multitudes of metamorphs may occur at these shores within 1–3 months. Maturity is reached in 2–4 years. Longevity in nature is not known, but marked toads estimated to be at least 10–11 years old occur at Oregon montane sites.

Natural History: These toads are generally nocturnal, especially in lowland areas. Breeding areas are often traditional locations, used year after year. Males have a "release call" (a series of short chirps like a chick: "pip-pip-pip") generally given in response to male-male interactions, such as being clasped by another male. Invertebrate prey of juvenile and adult toads includes insects, spiders, worms and slugs. Although the white, viscous skin toxin of the Western Toad (bufotoxin) deters many potential predators, some animals are not affected. Predators include gartersnakes, corvid birds (crows, ravens), Coyotes and Raccoons. These birds and mammals eviscerate adult toads, leaving the toxic skin. Larval predators also include sucking insects, such as predaceous diving beetles, that can penetrate the toxic skin of tadpoles. While eggs also have toxins and relatively few predators, they are susceptible to fungal infections. Disease may contribute to anuran population declines: chytrid fungal infection (phylum Chytridiomycota), an emerging wildlife infectious disease, has been documented in Western Toads.

Habitat: Breeding may occur in slow portions of streams, springs, ponds, lakes, reservoirs or stock ponds. Nonbreeding toadlets and adults occur in forest, woodland, grassland, meadow and desert and may be found near or far from water. Terrestrial microhabitat cover includes logs, stumps, vegetation, loose soil and rodent burrows. Overwintering hibernacula include burrows and subsurface retreats.

Remarks: Some sources refer to Western Toads as Boreal Toads. In the southern Rocky Mountains, particularly in Colorado and northern New Mexico, Western Toads cannot be found at > 80% of historic sites. In this region, the Western Toad is federally listed as a Candidate Species under the Endangered Species Act.

WOODHOUSE'S TOAD

Bufo woodhousii   GIRARD

Author: Lisa A. Hallock

Description: This is a medium to large terrestrial toad with a stout body, short legs, broad head, short, blunt snout and warty skin. Adults are 45–125 mm SVL. **The parotoid glands are elongate, and there are prominent, L-shaped cranial crests between and behind the eyes.** The cranial crests are absent in newly metamorphosed toads and are subtle in small juveniles. The ground color is gray, light brown or olive with dark blotches and spots. The underside is light colored with or without small, dark blotches. The pupil is horizontally oval. The dorsal stripe is white. There are two light-colored tubercles on the bottom of the hind feet. Males have a dark throat.

Eggs and Larvae: Eggs are laid in long strings. The largest clutch reported is 28,493

eggs from a 74 mm SVL female. The egg strings are laid in shallow water and are intertwined around vegetation or on the substrate. Individual eggs are small, colored black above and white below, with a single gelatinous envelope. The tadpole is small (around 25 mm TL at metamorphosis) and has a depressed body with dorsal eyes and a low fin that originates at the dorsal tail-body junction. The tip of the dorsal fin is rounded. The tadpole body and dorsal side of the tail musculature are darkly pigmented. Patches of white and golden pigment appear first near the underside of the tail base and increase over the surface of the body as the tadpole grows. The tail fin and underside of the tail musculature lack pigment but may have some dark flecking. Newly transformed toadlets are 10–13.5 mm SVL.

Similar Species: Prominent parotoid glands behind the head distinguish true toads from all other anurans. The Western Toad does not have cranial crests, and the parotoid glands are oval. Western Toad eggs have two gelatinous envelopes and usually appear to zigzag in a double row. Western Toad tadpoles are uniformly black or slate gray and have a dorsal fin that is moderately pigmented and a ventral fin that has little or no pigmentation. The abdomen has a fine golden shimmer in bright light. Rarely, individuals will have gold pigment that is more extensive, forming small blotches on the body and tail musculature.

Distribution: The Woodhouse's Toad is a North American species that occurs west of the Mississippi River in the United States and in north-central Mexico. In the region of this book, distribution is primarily in southeastern Washington along the Snake and Columbia Rivers. Woodhouse's Toads can also be found in southwestern Idaho, and in the Owyhee Reservoir, Malheur County, Oregon.

Adult male

Benton County,
Washington

Adult female

Benton County,
Washington

Adult

Benton County,
Washington

Underside of adult showing "seat patch" used to uptake water
Benton County, Washington

WILLIAM LEONARD

Tadpole
Benton County, Washington

WILLIAM LEONARD

Metamorph
Benton County, Washington

WILLIAM LEONARD

Life History: Woodhouse's Toads have a prolonged breeding season from late April through July. Breeding at individual sites may be much shorter, depending on water permanence. Development of the eggs is rapid, usually taking less than 10 days. Larval development takes approximately 2 months. Juveniles mature in 3 years, and adults may live for several years.

Natural History: Males arrive at the breeding sites before females and begin to call. The advertisement call is a loud, explosive, nasal "w-a-a-a-ah" lasting about 1–2.5 seconds. Individual females arrive throughout the breeding season, usually staying only one night to mate. Individual males come and go from the site, presumably to eat. Newly metamorphosed toadlets often gather on the edges of water bodies during the day. This species is terrestrial after metamorphosis, although Woodhouse's Toads tend to remain in the vicinity of water. They are active at night, starting at dusk. During the day, they shelter underground. Juvenile toads eat a variety of arthropods, including insects, spiders and mites. Adults are opportunistic feeders, with insects (primarily beetles) making up the majority of the diet. The warts and parotoid glands contain a toxin that is both distasteful and poisonous, making this species unpalatable to many predators. Bullfrogs have been observed to consume Woodhouse's Toads and then regurgitate them. Dexterous predators such as Raccoons are able to prey on this species by removing or avoiding the skin and parotoid glands.

Habitat: Terrestrial habitats include grassland and shrub-steppe. Egg-laying and larval development take place in a variety of permanent and temporary water bodies, including rain-filled pools, slow-flowing springs, ponds, sloughs and irrigation ditches.

Remarks: The eastern U.S. subspecies of the Woodhouse's Toad (*Bufo woodhousii fowleri*) is currently recognized as a distinct species, the Fowler's Toad (*Bufo fowleri*), based on advertisement call differences. When agitated, Woodhouse's Toads secrete a white poison from the "warts" (skin glands) and parotoid glands that is irritating to the mucous membranes of people and some animals. Dogs that lick or bite toads produce copious amounts of saliva in response to the toxin.

BOREAL CHORUS FROG

Pseudacris maculata   AGASSIZ

Author: Elke Wind

Description: The Boreal Chorus Frog is a relatively small amphibian, reaching a maximum of 40 mm snout to urostyle length (SUL). Females are slightly larger than males. This small frog has a pointed snout, short legs (the hind leg length = ⅓ SUL), and **dark lateral stripe extending from the tip of the snout to the groin on both sides.** Adults usually have a light-colored upper lip line. The species is highly variable in color, with a gray, tan or olive dorsum, overlaid with three darker stripes. The mid-dorsal stripe may be broken into patches or spots. Adults and juveniles often have a pale, triangular spot between the eyes. The ventral surface is cream or tan. Boreal Chorus Frogs have incomplete webbing between the toes of the hind limbs, they lack the dorsolateral folds that

are present in ranid frogs, and their skin is smooth dorsally and granular on the ventral surface. The tympanum is smaller than the eye. Newly metamorphosed Boreal Chorus Frogs are 7–12 mm in length. Juveniles are similar in appearance to adults, obtaining their dorsal stripes at metamorphosis.

Eggs and Larvae: Egg masses average 25 mm in diameter, with each 1.0 mm embryo dark above and light below. Masses containing 5–75 eggs are often found in a cluster along vegetative stems. Females usually lay 150–1500 eggs over several days. Hatchlings are gray and measure 4–7 mm in total length upon emergence. They have obvious, dark adhesive glands under the mouth. Tadpoles grow to 30 mm TL and are dark olive to black dorsally with gold speckles. Ventrally, they are gray with a coppery sheen. The eyes are spaced far apart on the head and break the body outline when viewed from above. The high, lightly mottled tail fin extends to the spiracle. The tail musculature is dark dorsally and light below. The anus opens to the right (dextral). The nostrils are prominent.

Similar Species: In northwestern North America, the Boreal Chorus Frog may be confused with the only other member of the chorus frog family, the Pacific Treefrog (*Pseudacris regilla*). Pacific Treefrogs can be larger (SUL to 50 mm) and have obvious pads on the tips of the toes used for climbing; the Boreal Chorus Frog lacks terminal toe pads. In contrast to the Boreal Chorus Frog, the Pacific Treefrog has a dark mask that is shorter, extending only to the shoulder. In addition, the hind limbs of Pacific Treefrogs are longer (lower length = ½ SUL). Pacific Treefrog egg masses are up to 40 mm in diameter.

Distribution: The Boreal Chorus Frog distribution extends beyond the scope of

Singing male
Glacier County, Montana

WILLIAM LEONARD

Adult male
Glacier County, Montana

WILLIAM LEONARD

Adult male
Glacier County, Montana

WILLIAM LEONARD

Singing male
*Glacier County,
Montana*

Egg mass
*Glacier County,
Montana*

Tadpole
*Fremont County,
Idaho*

this book, from east of the Continental Divide in the Yukon Territory and Montana to the east into Hudson's Bay and Wisconsin, and south into Arizona and New Mexico. In British Columbia, Boreal Chorus Frogs are found in the Peace River region in the northeastern part of the province, north of Prince George (54° N latitude). Only one population is found in the Yukon, near the La Biche River Valley in the southeast of the Territory. In Idaho, the Boreal Chorus Frog occurs in Caribou-Targhee National Forest as well as in the eastern half of the Snake River Plain; field studies are needed to assess the populations reported to occur in the Snake River Plain in southwestern Idaho.

Life History: Boreal Chorus Frogs breed in early spring, from approximately early May to late June in British Columbia. The eggs hatch in 10–14 days after egg-laying. Metamorphosis occurs approximately 2 months after hatching. Juvenile frogs reach sexual maturity in 1 year. Boreal Chorus Frogs may live for only 2–3 years.

Natural History: Males call from vegetative cover in both day and night, producing a rising trill that sounds much like a finger running down the tines of a comb. Like Wood Frogs, Boreal Chorus Frogs are freeze tolerant, flooding their cells with glucose in winter, which acts as a natural antifreeze. Adults and juveniles feed on a variety of invertebrates, such as ants, spiders, caterpillars, beetles, mites, springtails and flies.

Habitat: Within their extensive range, Boreal Chorus Frogs occur in many different habitats, including swamps, meadows, woodlands and open areas with sufficient cover. They breed in almost any water, shallow or deep, seeking submerged vegetation for egg-laying. Individual Boreal Chorus Frogs have been observed calling subterraneanly under drought conditions. Outside of the breeding season, individuals appear to spend the majority of their time on the surface or underground. As a result, little is known of their terrestrial habits. Boreal Chorus Frogs overwinter terrestrially.

Remarks: Prior to 1989, this animal was included as a subspecies of the Western Chorus Frog (also Striped Chorus Frog), *Pseudacris triseriata*. Most of what is known about this species comes from eastern parts of the range; little is known about western populations.

PACIFIC TREEFROG

Pseudacris regilla　　　　BAIRD AND GIRARD

Author: Gary M. Fellers

Description: Pacific Treefrogs are the most abundant frog in much of our region. Pacific Treefrogs are a small to medium-sized frog; adults range from 25–50 mm, while recently transformed individuals can be < 10 mm. **Dorsal coloration is highly variable (see Variation section below);** most individuals are a shade of brown or green. The back is often marked with an irregular pattern of dark, elongate spots or blotches. **Pacific Treefrogs are best identified by their expanded toe tips and an eye stripe that extends from the snout to the shoulder.** The chest and belly are creamy white. The underside of the legs is typically yellow. **Males have a dark throat** (cream-colored in females) that is greatly inflated while vocalizing.

Variation: This is a highly variable species, with the basic background color of juveniles and adults ranging from the typical brown or green to gray, tan, reddish, bronze or black. In some individuals, the dorsal markings are beautifully edged with copper or gold. Some individuals lack any dorsal pattern. Rarely, Pacific Treefrogs lack both dorsal markings and the eye stripe.

Eggs and Larvae: Pacific Treefrogs lay eggs in clusters of 10–80 eggs (typically 15–30). Each female may lay 20–30 egg clusters, totaling 500–750 (rarely > 1000) eggs. Clusters are attached to vegetation or almost any other object in shallow, still water. Each cluster is a soft, irregular mass that does not hold its shape out of the water, unlike California Newt egg masses. Larvae are various shades of dark brown to olive green, often with vague mottling or spotting. The ventral side is creamy white, typically with a metallic coppery or bronze sheen. Pacific Treefrog larvae are best identified by the position of their eyes, which are set well toward the side of the head so that they protrude beyond the outline of the head when viewed from above.

Similar Species: Boreal Chorus Frogs have an eye stripe (or dark mask) that continues past the shoulder to the groin; the eye stripe in Pacific Treefrogs stops at the shoulder. Also, Boreal Chorus Frogs do not have toe pads. These species occur together only in a small area of western Idaho. Foothill Yellow-legged Frogs can superficially resemble some treefrogs, but Foothill Yellow-legged Frogs do not have toe pads. Also, Foothill Yellow-legged Frogs have a dorsal-lateral fold beginning behind the eye and continuing partway toward the hind legs. Tailed frogs have cat-like vertical pupils, and males have a tail-like copulatory organ. Toad and true frog larvae have eyes set well in from the sides. Boreal Chorus Frog tadpoles are

Singing male
*Thurston County,
Washington*

WILLIAM LEONARD

**Red-colored female
at breeding pond**
*Pierce County,
Washington*

WILLIAM LEONARD

Pair in amplexus
*Thurston County,
Washington*

WILLIAM LEONARD

**Amplectic pair with
freshly laid eggs**
*King County,
Washington*

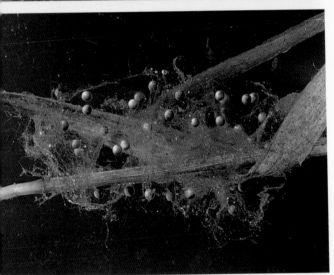

**Egg mass
attached to grass**
*Thurston County,
Washington*

Tadpole
*Pacific County,
Washington*

very similar to treefrogs, but their bodies are rounder, compared with the elliptical, potbellied shape of treefrog tadpoles.

Distribution: Pacific Treefrogs occur from central British Columbia to the southern tip of Baja California and from the Pacific Ocean east to western Montana, central Idaho, eastern Nevada and northwestern Arizona. Generally, they are absent from the California deserts. Pacific Treefrogs range from sea level to above timberline at 3550 m in the Sierra Nevada.

Life History: Pacific Treefrogs breed primarily in January and February; frogs in the mountains breed later, soon after snow melts from breeding sites. Eggs have been found every month from December through September. Eggs hatch in 2–3 weeks, and larvae spend 2–3 months before transforming into frogs, typically from June–August. While some individuals may breed when 1 year old, most do not reach maturity until their second year.

Natural History: Treefrogs call in large, loud choruses. Unlike most frogs, they often call throughout much of the day during the peak of breeding. Since most frogs in the Pacific Northwest produce only weak and rarely heard vocalizations or do not call at all, Pacific Treefrogs are the most commonly heard species in our region. Male Pacific Treefrogs defend calling territories by using specialized vocalizations and by fighting. Fighting frogs butt with their heads, kick with their feet and jump on each other in an attempt to displace competing males. Daytime calling apparently serves to establish males at preferred sites for the evening. Larval Pacific Treefrogs feed on small organisms suspended in the water: algae, diatoms and bacteria, as well as organic and non-organic detritus. Adults feed on almost any small invertebrate that they can ingest, including insects, spiders, isopods and snails. Pacific Treefrog predators include fish, snakes, herons, egrets, Raccoons, skunks, River Otters and larger frogs. During metamorphosis, many individuals are consumed by gartersnakes.

Habitat: Pacific Treefrogs breed in nearly any freshwater habitat, including ponds, marshes, ditches, reservoirs, lakes and the slower stretches of streams. Like most frogs, treefrogs breed most abundantly in fishless bodies of water. During the non-breeding season, treefrogs can be found in almost any slightly moist habitat: under rocks or logs, down animal burrows and in riparian corridors, woodlands and grasslands, as well as in ponds, marshes and streams.

Remarks: This species is sometimes placed in the genus *Hyla*.

NORTHERN RED-LEGGED FROG

Rana aurora   BAIRD AND GIRARD

Authors: Kelly R. McAllister and William P. Leonard

Description: Adults and juveniles have a dark eye-mask, **red under-legs** and **colorful greenish or sometimes reddish groin mottling.** Red pigment may be confined to the undersides of the lower legs and thighs or include the margins of the underbelly, often in a "U" shape. Red pigment is often lacking on the undersides of juveniles. Dorsally, adults and juveniles are usually tan or brown and **marked with black flecks or small spots.** The throat and chest are frequently pigmented with a suffusion of dark gray or black peppering. The **heel extends beyond the nostrils** when the hind limb is adpressed forward. Iris color is brown or gold. Females measure to about 100 mm in body length, while males may reach about 70 mm.

Variation: Northern Red-legged Frogs occasionally have extensive black spotting and sometimes none at all. Spots occasionally form "rosettes" that resemble the light-centered spots typical of the Oregon Spotted Frog.

Eggs and Larvae: Eggs are laid in a roughly round mass composed of 750–2000 eggs, measuring 76–152 mm in diameter. Individual eggs, inclusive of jelly envelopes, range 10–14 mm in diameter; the loose jelly layer streams through one's fingers when picked up. At early developmental stages, each egg is black on top and white or cream colored below, and 2–3.5 mm in diameter. Small tadpoles, 10–20 mm in length, have parallel light lines on either side of the mid-dorsal line. Older tadpoles are tan or dark brown dorsally and off-white or gold-mottled ventrally; gold- or brass-colored flecks form coarse mottling on the sides. The tail musculature and fin of tadpoles are usually marked with dark spots.

Similar Species: Spotted frogs, both Oregon and Columbia, lack the colorful groin patch and have yellow or chartreuse eyes. Cascades Frogs are yellow underneath and lack the colorful groin patch. Tadpoles are difficult or impossible to distinguish reliably from those of spotted and Cascades Frogs. Because of range overlap, Northern Red-legged Frog tadpoles are most likely to be confused with those of the Oregon Spotted Frog and Cascades Frog, both of which have finer, silvery flecking on the sides, contrasted with the coarse, gold or brassy pigments on the sides of Northern Red-legged Frog tadpoles. Bullfrogs also overlap greatly in geographic range and may be confused at small size. Large Bullfrog tadpoles have yellow, opaque underbellies and gray or green dorsa with regularly spaced, round, black spots. Pacific Treefrog tadpoles can be readily distinguished by viewing from above; the eyes of the treefrogs protrude beyond the

Adult
*Thurston County,
Washington*

WILLIAM LEONARD

Adult
*Pacific County,
Washington*

WILLIAM LEONARD

**Pair in amplexis
showing colorful
groin patch**
*Pierce County,
Washington*

WILLIAM LEONARD

Pair in amplexis
*King County,
Washington*

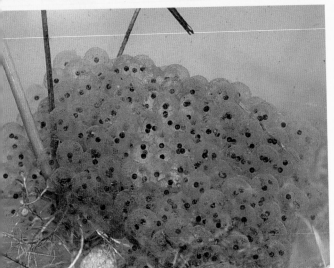

Egg mass
*Fraser Valley,
British Columbia*

Tadpole
*Thurston County,
Washington*

margin of the outline of the head, while the eyes of the Northern Red-legged Frog are slightly within the margin.

Distribution: The Northern Red-legged Frog is largely coastal in distribution, extending from southern British Columbia south to north of Elk, Mendocino County, California. It occurs at mid-elevations along the west slopes of the Cascade Range and penetrates slightly east of the crest at lower mountain passes and along the Columbia River. A population in southeast Alaska was introduced by a local teacher.

Life History: Breeding occurs from December to February at coastal locations but is delayed until March at more northerly and higher elevation sites. Eggs hatch in several weeks, and the small, gilled hatchlings cling to vegetation, living off of yolk reserves for several days before beginning to swim about grazing on algae and detritus. By mid- to late summer, Red-legged Frog tadpoles develop all four legs and complete their transformation into small frogs. In their first summer, Northern Red-legged Frogs range from 20–30 mm SVL. Males begin to breed just prior to 2 years of age, while females breed at the age of 3 years.

Natural History: In the fall of the year, males sometimes make an advertisement call similar to that given during the breeding season. Cold weather drives them to shelter underground or back to water. During the breeding season, males develop nuptial pads on the "thumbs," which aid in clasping females during breeding. In late winter, adults congregate in suitable breeding sites, which consist of ponds and wetlands with relatively dense, emergent vegetation. Males advertise their positions with a succession of 3–7 low grunts or clucks, which are generally given below the water's surface. When a receptive female swims near enough, she is clasped by the male immediately behind the front legs in a nuptial embrace referred to as amplexus. Eggs are fertilized externally by the male as they are extruded into the water by the female; egg masses are attached to aquatic vegetation just below the water's surface in water up to 60 cm deep. There is no evidence that an individual female lays more than a single egg mass per season. The diet of tadpoles is poorly studied but likely consists of plankton, algae and other plant material. Transformed Northern Red-legged Frogs eat a variety of terrestrial arthropods; they are preyed upon by gartersnakes, Mink and herons. Northern Red-legged Frogs emit an extended, loud, high-pitched shriek when seized by a gartersnake. The purpose of such "alarm calls" is puzzling since gartersnakes lack hearing; perhaps these calls serve to alert nearby frogs of danger.

Habitat: Northern Red-legged Frogs are found within forested regions, and adults often spend the non-breeding season in forests with diverse understories of woody shrubs and herbaceous vegetation. For breeding, Northern Red-legged Frogs require shallow ponds, slow-moving streams with marshy edges, or extensive wetlands with relatively stable water levels.

Remarks: Northern Red-legged Frogs are relatively common throughout most of their range. In coastal regions, the only frog likely to be more widespread and abundant is the Pacific Treefrog. In many wetlands, lakes and ponds, Northern Red-legged Frogs appear able to co-exist with the non-native Bullfrog, something that may be dependent upon the availability of more complex aquatic habitats, both in terms of water depths and vegetation. The two red-legged frog species are sometimes recognized as subspecies, the Northern Red-legged Frog (*Rana aurora aurora*) and the California Red-legged Frog (*R. aurora draytonii*).

FOOTHILL YELLOW-LEGGED FROG

Rana boylii   BAIRD

Authors: Marc P. Hayes, Sarah J. Kupferberg and Amy J. Lind

Description: The Foothill Yellow-legged Frog is **the smallest native ranid frog in the Pacific Northwest,** reaching a size up to 82 mm and weighing up to 45 g. Dorsal color usually appears beige, brown or gray, with somewhat warty or rough upper skin surfaces. This textured skin almost conceals **small eardrums and weak dorsolateral folds.** Toes are completely webbed, and undersides of the hind limbs are cream to bright yellow. Female body size is about 16 mm larger than that of males. Males have enlarged forelimbs, a rough black or gray nuptial pad on each thumb and a generally slimmer appearance. Juveniles look similar to females and typically have more contrasting colors,

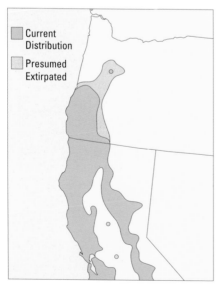

Current Distribution

Presumed Extirpated

and the yellow wash on undersurfaces is weak or absent.

Variation: Dorsal color is variable. Frogs may be brick red or have irregularly placed brick red spots, or they may be uniformly gray or brown to contrastingly light and dark mottled. The yellow undersurface intensifies with age; yellow may be present only on the lower legs or feet in juveniles but may extend over hind limb undersurfaces and onto most of the belly in the largest frogs. The latter individuals also often have a hint of orange on the yellow thighs. Marbling may occur on an otherwise white throat. One albino has been reported.

Eggs and Larvae: Eggs are medium-sized (1.9–2.4 mm in diameter), black on top grading to off-white below. Grape-like egg masses are attached to hard substrates in gently flowing water. Egg masses vary roughly from the size of a small orange to that of a grapefruit (75–150 mm); small masses can have < 400 eggs, but large ones can have >1500 eggs. Tadpoles at least 25 mm in length have dorsally located eyes, with a relatively flattened body, a thick, muscular tail with a reduced fin area, and a well-developed, downward-oriented mouth. Tadpole color is typically olive to beige. Distinct dark spotting in a diffuse pattern is often present on the tail muscles and fin; the body may have more subtle dark spotting. Gold flecking is scattered over the tail and upper body surfaces. The lower body surface is opaque silvery white to pale yellow, making the intestines only faintly visible. Tadpoles can reach 50–70 mm TL and develop 12–13 rows of teeth before metamorphosis.

Similar Species: Western and Woodhouse's Toads have shorter legs (giving them a walking or short-hopping gait), a pale, narrow, mid-dorsal stripe and a prominent gland behind each eye. Other true frogs native to our area have more distinct dorsolateral folds and less extensive

Adult
*Linn County,
Oregon*

Underside of an adult
*Linn County,
Oregon*

Adult
*Linn County,
Oregon*

Egg mass
Linn County,
Oregon

Tadpole
Linn County,
Oregon

Juvenile
Linn County,
Oregon

toe webbing. Juvenile Bullfrogs may be about the size of adult Foothill Yellow-legged Frogs, but they usually have green on the head, lack dorsolateral folds and chirp when they jump. Cascades Frogs, some Columbia Spotted Frogs and juvenile California Red-legged Frogs have a yellow wash on undersurfaces, but all have dark facial masks, prominent light lip stripes and smooth skin.

Distribution: Foothill Yellow-legged Frogs historically ranged from the Santiam River in Oregon south to the San Gabriel River in southern California, with an isolated population in the Sierra San Pedro Mártir, Baja California. Foothill Yellow-legged Frogs are largely gone from the southern third and most of the northern part of their range. In the Willamette Valley, Oregon, Foothill Yellow-legged Frogs reach 415 m in elevation, and in northwestern California, they have been recorded up to 1341 m. In Mexico, they reach 2042 m (La Grulla Meadow, Baja California).

Life History: The life history of Foothill Yellow-legged Frogs is closely linked to stream hydrology. Males gather near egg-laying sites. Egg-laying occurs in spring (March–June), usually when stream flows have declined to a level where scour is less likely. Egg masses are usually laid on rock in the shallows of the relatively broader channels in medium-sized or larger streams at water temperatures of 8–20°C. After egg-laying, females leave breeding sites, but males seem to remain for a few weeks. Hatching occurs in 10–28 days. Young larvae remain in low-flow areas and become tolerant of somewhat higher-flow velocities as they grow. Larvae graze on attached algae and diatoms that develop as a film on rocks. Metamorphosis typically occurs in low-flow backwaters 4–5 months after hatching. Size at metamorphosis is 18–28 mm. Males reach reproductive age in about

a year (40 mm), but females may need 2 years. This frog lives only 5–6 years.

Natural History: Historically, stream processes and native predators were probably the key factors influencing Foothill Yellow-legged Frog natural history. Predators include gartersnakes, dragonfly larvae and water bug larvae. Minor predators include other insects, birds, fishes and mammals.

Habitat: Foothill Yellow-legged Frogs require streams large enough to develop bar and backwater habitat for reproduction and larval rearing. They also require coarse substrate with interstitial spaces for refugia. Small, higher-gradient streams or tributaries usually lack such habitat, may scour more frequently and have temperatures that may be too cool for reproduction. Small tributaries may be an important summer refuge when the open habitat of the larger streams used for reproduction becomes too hot. Overwintering habitat requirements are poorly understood, but small tributaries may represent important overwintering areas for these frogs.

Remarks: In Oregon, Foothill Yellow-legged Frogs have vanished from over 50% of historic sites. In California, greater losses may have occurred. In particular, the species now appears to be extremely rare south of San Francisco Bay in both the coastal ranges and the foothills of the Sierra Nevada, where it was formerly abundant and widespread in low-gradient streams. Changes in stream processes due to manipulation of streams for various reasons (e.g., dams) and the introduction of novel aquatic predators are thought to be key factors in these declines.

CASCADES FROG

Rana cascadae   SLATER

Author: Deanna H. Olson

Description: Adults typically have numerous, well-defined, **inky black dorsal spots. A yellow upper jaw (lip) stripe extends almost to the shoulder.** A dark mask crosses the eye and tympanic membrane, and the **eye orients outward.** The iris is gold. Dorsolateral folds extend down each side of the back to the hip. Toe webbing does not extend to the last segment of the longest hind toe. Dorsal color can be tan, reddish brown, or brown to olive green. **Ventral color is cream to yellow, with ventral hind limbs being yellow to honey colored.** The groin is mottled with contrasting light (cream, yellow or greenish yellow) and dark (gray, greenish to brown) patches. Females are larger (to approximately 75 mm SVL) than males (to 60 mm SVL). During the breeding season, males' thumbs have nuptial

pads. Metamorphs (10–25 mm SVL) are more uniformly olive green to brown, with a rough appearance to the skin, and usually lack black dorsal spotting.

Variation: Dorsal color may vary, and dorsal spots may be lacking. Distinct populations have been described genetically: California Cascades Frogs differ markedly from more northerly populations in Oregon and Washington; in Washington, a lesser degree of divergence is apparent between animals in the Olympic Peninsula and the Cascade Range.

Eggs and Larvae: The egg mass is initially the size of a golf ball, but the jelly quickly absorbs water to become grapefruit-sized (80–150 mm; 300–500 eggs). Eggs are two-toned: black when viewed from the top and white underneath. Egg clutches may be oviposited singly or in communal masses from 2 to > 50 clutches. With time, egg masses spread out, communal masses coalesce and algae may grow on the outer surface. At first, hatchlings are largely immobile at egg masses. They are dark brown to black, with a nearly opaque dorsal fin. They are 4–6 mm long and have external gills and long tails that are > 1.5 times the body length. Free-swimming larvae are brown to brownish black with silver to gold flecking on their sides and ventral surface. The dorsal fin is dark and translucent. Larvae may form loose aggregations, usually with < 100 individuals.

Similar Species: Cascades Frog eggs, larvae, juveniles and adults may be particularly difficult to distinguish from sympatric ranids without close inspection. Spotted frogs and Northern Red-legged Frogs often have pink or red on their ventral surface, and their dorsal spots have indistinct edges. Spotted frogs have relatively shorter hind legs; the heel of a hind leg adpressed along the body does not extend to the snout as it does in the Cascades and Northern Red-legged Frogs.

Adult
Pierce County,
Washington

Adult
Grays Harbor County,
Washington

Underside of an adult
Skagit County,
Washington

Adult
*Skagit County,
Washington*

WILLIAM LEONARD

Egg mass
*King County,
Washington*

KLAUS O. RICHTER

Tadpole
*Klickitat County,
Washington*

WILLIAM LEONARD

The spotted frog groin has pale patterning. Spotted frog eyes are oriented upward, and their irises are a brighter yellow to chartreuse. The Northern Red-legged Frog groin has mottled patches that are larger than those occurring more forward on their bodies. Foothill Yellow-legged Frogs have indistinct dorsolateral folds. Tailed frogs have no dorsolateral folds, and they have vertical pupils and flattened, outermost hind toes. Northwestern Salamander eggs look similar but are very firm masses that retain their round shape when lifted out of the water; they also are attached to vegetation or wood. In contrast, Cascades Frog egg masses are more flaccid and are unattached to vegetation.

Distribution: This is a mountain frog endemic to the Northwest, occurring above about 610 m elevation. It is distributed across several disjunct montane areas: the Olympic Peninsula, the Cascade Range of Oregon and Washington, the California Shasta-Trinity and Marble Mountains, and an area near Lassen Peak, California.

Life History: Breeding occurs from March to July as the snow melts at breeding ponds. Breeding is explosive, with most pairs ovipositing over a few days, although "straggler" pairs may continue to breed for a couple of weeks. During breeding, adult males congregate in a small area of a pond, positioned at the water's surface. When a male detects a frog nearby on the surface, he produces a repeated call, "chuck-chuck-chuck," approaches and attempts to clasp the detected frog. This call also may be used as a "release call," used by a male when clasped by another male. Females have been observed approaching the breeding site by swimming underwater, and upon surfacing near males, were soon clasped. Egg masses are deposited in shallow water (approximately 15 cm deep), not attached to vegetation. Hatching occurs in a few days to a couple of weeks. Metamorphosis occurs within 1–3 months. It is estimated that frogs breed at age 3–4 years. Some frogs live to be more than 6 years old.

Natural History: Breeding sites are traditional areas used year after year. Juveniles and adults often are found at sites that have no evidence of breeding, suggesting that their home ranges span more than one aquatic site. After breeding, Cascades Frogs may use nearby ponds and creeks as summer foraging habitat, refugia and stepping stones or corridors for dispersal. Although the spatial scale at which populations function is not known, genetic analyses show low gene flow at distances > 10 km. Tadpole predators are many, including predaceous diving beetles, dragonfly larvae, birds such as American Robins and Clark's Nutcrackers, Rough-skinned Newts, Northwestern Salamanders, and exotic fishes such as Brook Trout. Brook Trout and newts also eat the eggs. After metamorphosis, Cascades Frogs may become prey for birds (e.g., Common Ravens) and mammals. Tadpoles are primarily bottom-feeders, grazing on algae and detritus at the bottom of ponds. After metamorphosis, Cascades Frogs eat invertebrates.

Habitat: This frog is usually found near water. Breeding occurs in shallow water of ephemeral ponds, deep areas or pothole pools within flooded mountain meadows, lake shores, off-channel pools of streams, and pond habitats of anthropogenic origin such as roadside ditches and forest pond impoundments used for dust or fire control. Beyond the breeding season, juveniles and adults are found in a broader array of habitats, including meadows, ponds and lakes not used for breeding. They are also found along streams and creeks and in seeps.

Remarks: Population declines of Cascades Frogs have been noted in California. Causes of losses may be site-specific and may include fish-stocking, drought, pathogens and habitat degradation.

BULLFROG

Rana catesbeiana   SHAW

Authors: Marc P. Hayes and Mark R. Jennings

Description: The Bullfrog is **the largest North American frog** (to 229 mm SVL and over 1.4 kg). It has **large eardrums,** fully webbed feet and **no dorsolateral folds.** Bullfrogs nearly always show **light and dark marbling under the thighs** and some green on the head. Males have a yellow throat, enormous eardrums, enlarged forearms and dark nuptial pads on their thumbs. Females have smaller eardrums and lack enlarged forearms, nuptial pads or a yellow throat. Juvenile Bullfrogs look like females but have a brighter green coloration.

Variation: Dorsal color is green, brown, rust or a combination of two or more of these colors. Marbling on undersurfaces may occur only on the thighs, extend across the undersurfaces or be absent (rarely).

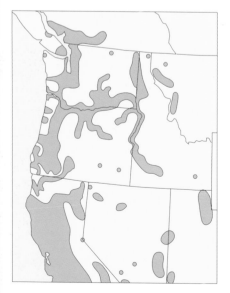

Albino, blue or yellow Bullfrogs have been found but are rare in the wild.

Eggs and Larvae: Eggs are tiny (< 1 mm in diameter) and are colored dark above and cream below. The egg mass is a large sheet laid on the water surface with 4000–78,000 eggs in it. At hatching, tadpoles are dark, with a yellowish cream belly. At 25 mm, tadpoles have eyes placed relatively high on the head, gold flecking and black dots on the body and intestines visible through the belly. Larger tadpoles (to 170 mm TL) are bicolored, khaki green with black dots above and yellow concealing the intestines below.

Similar Species: Green Frogs look similar but are much smaller (108 mm SVL maximum) and have dorsolateral folds. All other true frogs in the Pacific Northwest have dorsolateral folds, a smaller maximum size (to 111 mm in the largest), and, except for Northern Leopard Frog, rarely have any green. Green Frogs lay a similar egg mass but have fewer eggs (1000–5000), and larger eggs (approximately 1.5 mm in diameter). Pacific Treefrogs have similar-sized eggs, but these are laid underwater in small oblong packets of < 100. All other Pacific Northwest amphibians that reproduce in aquatic habitats also lay their eggs underwater and either have larger eggs or an ovoid mass or packet. Green Frog tadpoles are similar except that they are cream below with a coppery sheen and have a smaller maximum size (≤ 100 mm). All other tadpoles of Pacific Northwest amphibians lack black dots scattered on a greenish background or have laterally placed eyes.

Distribution: Bullfrogs are generally found at lower elevations in the Pacific Northwest but range to higher elevations at more southern locales. In British Columbia, Bullfrogs occur up to 366 m, whereas in southern Oregon, they are recorded up to 1480 m.

Portrait of an adult female
Thurston County, Washington

Adult female
Thurston County, Washington

Adult male
King County, Washington

**Underside
of an adult**
*Thurston County,
Washington*

WILLIAM LEONARD

Tadpole
*Klickitat County,
Washington*

WILLIAM LEONARD

Juvenile
*Clark County,
Washington*

WILLIAM LEONARD

Life History: Bullfrogs require warm-water habitats. Males call at water temperatures $\geq 20°C$, and reproduction occurs at $\geq 21.1°C$. Breeding begins in May or June in the Pacific Northwest. Hatching occurs in 6 days to 2 weeks. Food and temperature influence rate of development. Tadpoles usually overwinter at least once. Broad variation exists in metamorphic size (25–67 mm). Metamorphosed individuals typically mature in 2–3 years at most Pacific Northwest sites. In south-central Washington, males mature around 105 mm SVL; females mature at a slightly larger 115 mm SVL. In the Pacific Northwest, longevity is unknown; elsewhere, Bullfrogs are short-lived (less than 8 years).

Natural History: During breeding, males give a loud, low-pitched call that sounds like "jug-o-rum" or "bwum, bwum, bwum." Despite this obvious call, males are often hard to find because calls are ventriloquial, and calling often occurs from hidden locations. Eggs are usually laid within males' territories, and females may reproduce more than once seasonally. When disturbed, juveniles may "chirp" as they leap into the water. A large size, a voracious appetite, ability to use human-altered aquatic habitats (including the ability to tolerate polluted conditions), a capability for moving long distances (more than 1.6 km), a number of eggs (per mass) much larger than any other amphibian and the potential to reproduce more than once annually would seem to make Bullfrogs a problem as an introduction to the Pacific Northwest. However, no regional studies to date have succeeded in clearly identifying Bullfrogs as a problem. Bullfrog traits allow them to do well in fish-rich, warm-water habitats. Human-altered habitats in the Pacific Northwest are often rich in introduced fishes and have warmer water. These conditions tend to disfavor native amphibians, so the effects that Bullfrogs may have on the native fauna are hard to distinguish from those of introduced fishes and other habitat alterations. Disentangling these effects remains a challenge to understanding the actual impact of the Bullfrog in the Pacific Northwest.

Habitat: Bullfrogs need permanent water for reproduction, rearing of tadpoles and active-season survival of juveniles and adults. Juvenile Bullfrogs can use diverse aquatic habitats, but reproduction requires permanent warm water. Therefore, reproductive habitat must be stillwater with suitably high temperatures for at least 5 months. Water depth and cover requirements for overwintering adults are unknown. However, in the Midwest and South, adult Bullfrogs seem to prefer aquatic habitats with some vegetation and deep (> 60 cm) water. Larval and first-year frogs tend to prefer sun-exposed, vegetated, shallow water.

Remarks: Bullfrogs were first introduced to the Pacific Northwest in 1895. Most stock came from the first successful regional introduction at Boise, Idaho, and via overland express from New Orleans dealers. Bullfrogs were imported for food, but immigrants from the South or Midwest also introduced Bullfrogs out of nostalgia for their calls. A frog-farming craze (1920–1940) followed, when many hoped to become rich raising frogs. All ventures failed, and would-be farmers either let their stock disperse or scattered Bullfrogs around the countryside.

GREEN FROG

Rana clamitans   LATREILLE

Author: Herbert A. Brown

Description: This stout, medium-sized frog is green, olive or brown dorsally, occasionally marked by a few round spots on the back and sides, dusky bars across the legs and a broad, light green jaw stripe. The ventral surface is creamy white to yellow, occasionally with gray mottling partway down the abdomen. The **prominent dorso-lateral folds extend over each tympanum and about two-thirds of the way down the back.** The **male has a conspicuous tympanum** that is approximately twice the diameter of the eye, and the throat is yellow. The female's tympanum is about the same diameter as the eye, and the throat is cream colored. All toes of the hind feet are fully webbed except the outer toe, which is partially webbed. Females may reach 100 mm in length; males may reach

95 mm. Unlike most frogs, where females are markedly larger than males, female and male Green Frogs are often equal in size; the large size of males probably correlates with the development of aggressive territorial defense by males during breeding season. Newly transformed froglets measure about 23–28 mm in length.

Variation: Sometimes frogs with a blue color in the skin can be found, but these are unusual. These frogs lack pigment cells that produce a yellow hue in the upper skin layer, creating a bluish tint.

Eggs and Larvae: Each female lays from 1000–5000 eggs (egg diameter, 1.5 mm) in a large, loose mass that floats among aquatic vegetation at the water's surface. The tadpoles are large (64 mm). The upper body and tail are colored olive green to brown with dark blotches. On the lower side of the body, tadpoles are cream colored with a slight coppery iridescence. The tail is relatively long, with an acute tip, and the dorsal fin begins slightly behind the base of the tail-trunk boundary.

Similar Species: The adult Bullfrog has a larger body size and lacks a dorsolateral fold. The Bullfrog tadpole is larger, with skin color dominated by a green hue and the presence of conspicuous black dots.

Distribution: This introduced frog is native to the eastern and maritime provinces of Canada and to much of the eastern half of the United States. Green Frogs are known to occur at three localities in Washington: Lake Washington (elevation 209 m) in King County, Toad Lake (elevation 225 m) in Whatcom County and Lake Gillette (elevation 960 m) in Stevens County. In British Columbia, Green Frogs are widespread throughout the Lower Fraser Valley. There are also several locality records from southern and eastern Vancouver Island. The species appears to be patchily distributed on the island. It is unknown whether Green

Singing male
Ingham County, Michigan

Adult female
Whatcom County, Washington

**Portrait of
an adult male**
*Ingham County,
Michigan*

Egg mass
*Ingham County,
Michigan*

Tadpole
*Whatcom County,
Washington*

Frogs are expanding their range in British Columbia.

Life History: Breeding activity begins with the onset of warm temperatures in the late spring or early summer and probably extends into August. Embryonic development is rapid, and hatchling tadpoles may emerge from egg capsules in less than a week. Eggs and tadpoles are adapted for development in relatively warm waters, but in northern populations where environmental temperatures are lower, the tadpoles grow more slowly, generally requiring 2 years until transformation into juvenile frogs. Tadpoles transform into small froglets in late summer in areas where egg-laying occurs early in the year. In areas where eggs are laid late in the breeding season, tadpoles may transform into larger-sized froglets sometime during the next summer. Green Frogs may live several years.

Natural History: Adult Green Frogs are highly aquatic, seldom leaving a body of permanent, standing water. During breeding, males call while slightly submerged in the water either on or among aquatic vegetation. The male's single-note, low-pitched croak has been compared aptly to the sound made by plucking the lowest string of a banjo. This advertisement call serves to attract potential mates and to warn rival males. Males vigorously defend prime breeding sites from intruding males, and wrestling matches are common. During rainy weather, juveniles reportedly disperse into adjacent woods and fields. Green Frogs feed primarily on aquatic insects and other invertebrates but also will prey upon tadpoles and newly transformed frogs. The tadpoles feed primarily on algae and other vegetation. Green Frogs are eaten by gartersnakes and a variety of birds and mammals.

Habitat: In their native range, Green Frogs live in a variety of aquatic habitats, including lakes, ponds, swamps and the margins of streams. Adults commonly hibernate beneath logs or leaf debris, while the tadpoles spend the winter at the bottom of the pond.

Remarks: This frog, like the Bullfrog, is an introduced species in the Pacific Northwest. It was probably accidentally introduced in the tadpole stage with a sample of Bullfrog tadpoles (perhaps in a failed attempt to farm Bullfrogs for frog legs) or with fish (such as bass or perch) transplanted to a pond or lake. There is some information that the population at Toad Lake might have originated in the year 1910; the Bullfrog also inhabits this lake. It is not known to what extent Green Frogs pose a threat to native amphibians. However, in light of the potential threats that the Bullfrog and other non-native species may pose to native species, further introductions are strongly discouraged. The Green Frog is commonly used in research. It is often used in laboratories to study the influence of pesticides or parasites (e.g., leeches) on embryonic and tadpole development. The Green Frog has been used to study rates of colonization and invasion of new habitats following historical glacial periods in the Midwest (Iowa). They have also been used to study sensory modes (smell, hearing and vision) and environmental cues that amphibians use to orient their movements and migrations.

CALIFORNIA RED-LEGGED FROG

Rana draytonii   BAIRD AND GIRARD

Author: Gary M. Fellers

Description: The California Red-legged Frog is the **largest native frog in the Pacific Northwest,** with adults ranging 45–130 mm in length. They are best identified by **a conspicuous dorsolateral fold** that runs along each side, from the eye to the base of the hind legs. Dorsally, adults are medium to dark brown, often with some reddish coloration, especially toward the posterior. There are usually irregular dark blotches on the back and dark bars on the hind legs. Most individuals have a cream-colored stripe along the upper jaw; this is most distinct in smaller individuals. The **color of the underside is cream with varying amounts of red.** Sometimes the legs and entire chest are brick red. Young frogs and some adults lack red entirely.

Variation: Dorsal coloration ranges from a pale, yellowish brown to brick red. It is not unusual to find frogs of all color variations at a single pond. Average and maximum size varies geographically; frogs near the coast are smaller than frogs only 25 km inland.

Eggs and Larvae: Females lay a single mass of eggs containing 300–4000 eggs (average about 2000) that typically hatch in 10–14 days. Egg masses are irregular (like a cluster of grapes) and soft. Typically, they are attached to emergent vegetation near the water surface. Tadpoles have eyes set well in from the outline of the head. Dorsal color is usually brownish with darker marbling, but color variations include gray, olive and greenish. Ventrally, tadpoles have a pinkish iridescence.

Similar Species: California Red-legged Frogs are probably indistinguishable from Northern Red-legged Frogs in the field. The two species of red-legged frog should be identified by geographic distribution. Those found along the coast north of Elk (Mendocino County, California) are Northern Red-legged Frogs, while those south or east of a line from Point Arena (Mendocino County) to Redding (Shasta County) are California Red-legged Frogs. Coastal frogs between Elk and Point Arena could be either species. Most Cascades Frogs differ from red-legged frogs by having sharply defined black dorsal markings and a yellowish color on the lower abdomen and underside of the legs. Cascades Frogs have a more rounded snout and often a much whiter and more conspicuous jaw stripe. This is especially prevalent in young frogs. Also, Cascades Frogs occur at much higher elevations than California Red-legged Frogs. In fact, currently, these two species are not known to coexist. Bullfrogs lack a dorsolateral fold and are never reddish on the back. Partly submerged Bullfrogs with only their heads out of the water can resemble red-

Adult
*Marin County,
California*

GARY FELLERS

Adult
*Marin County,
California*

GARY FELLERS

Underside of an adult
*Marin County,
California*

WILLIAM LEONARD

Adult
Marin County,
California

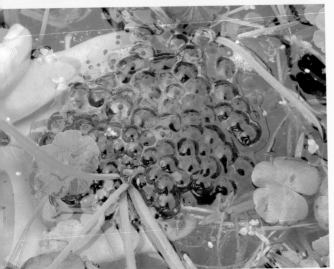

Egg mass
Marin County,
California

Tadpole
Monterey County,
California

legged frogs, but Bullfrogs have greenish (not brown) snouts. Foothill Yellow-legged Frogs lack a well-defined dorsolateral fold but might otherwise be confused with young California Red-legged Frogs that lack red on their legs. Red-leg disease (caused by *Aeromonas* bacteria) can cause the capillaries on the underside of the legs of any frog to dilate, producing a reddish color that might be confused with the red coloration of a California Red-legged Frog. California Red-legged Frog tadpoles lack the distinct, fine black spots found on Bullfrog larvae. The eyes of treefrog larvae protrude beyond the margin of the head.

Distribution: Along the coast, California Red-legged Frogs range from 15 km north of Point Arena, California, south to the Sierra San Pedro Mártir, Baja California. There are major gaps in the range in southern California where urbanization has greatly reduced suitable habitat. Only four sites are currently known in the Sierra Nevada foothills. The floor of the Central Valley probably never supported California Red-legged Frogs, due to extensive flooding that occurs during winter storms and spring runoff.

Life History: The timing of breeding varies geographically. Coastal populations in central and northern California breed primarily in January, while more inland and southern populations breed into late March. Locally, peak breeding takes place over a 2–3 week period. Larvae typically metamorphose in 3.5–7 months; newly transformed froglets are 16–20 mm. Occasionally, tadpoles overwinter and metamorphose after 14–16 months. Frogs begin breeding when they are 2–3 years old, and they may live 8–10 years.

Natural History: Males vocalize both underwater and at the water surface, though they are often quiet, even on nights with lots of breeding activity. In addition to the low-pitched advertisement/territorial call given by males, frogs of both sexes often give a release call when grasped. Most striking is a rarely heard "scream" that seems to function as a mechanism to startle predators. Rough-skinned Newts feed on the eggs of red-legged frogs. Opossums, Raccoons, skunks, Great Blue Herons, American Bitterns, Black-crowned Night-Herons, Red-shouldered Hawks, gartersnakes, Bullfrogs, various native and non-native species of fish and crayfish eat the tadpoles or frogs.

Habitat: California Red-legged Frogs breed in both seasonal and permanent ponds or marshes, or in the quiet, pond-like parts of streams. Less commonly, they breed in lakes or other large bodies of water. Stock ponds are commonly used, sometimes even when heavily impacted by livestock. Breeding sites typically have emergent vegetation, but frogs occasionally breed in ponds entirely devoid of vegetation. Many individuals spend most of the year well away from breeding areas, with some frogs leaving shortly after breeding. Other frogs remain at breeding ponds all year or leave just as the pond dries up. Non-breeding habitat includes riparian corridors and dense thickets with at least a small amount of surface water. Along the coast, California Red-legged Frogs can be found in forests that are kept moist by summer fog drip.

Remarks: The California Red-legged Frog was once abundant throughout much of its range. Now the species is nearly gone in both the Sierra Nevada foothills and along the southern California coast. The largest populations occur in the vicinity of San Francisco Bay and near Half Moon Bay. Because the frog is threatened by a wide variety of human activities, it was federally listed as a Threatened Species in 1996. Both red-legged frog species are sometimes recognized as subspecies: Northern Red-legged Frog (*Rana aurora aurora*) and California Red-legged Frog (*R. aurora draytonii*).

COLUMBIA SPOTTED FROG

Rana luteiventris   THOMPSON

Authors: William P. Leonard and Evelyn L. Bull

Description: The Columbia Spotted Frog is brown, olive green, tan or gray dorsally. Irregularly shaped black spots with light centers mark the back and legs. The undersides are cream colored, overlaid with apricot, salmon or yellow pigment on the hind legs and abdomen; gray pigment can also be present on the throat and lower abdomen. **The groin lacks prominent mottling. Eyes are markedly upturned.** A dorsolateral fold runs along each side of the back. **The hind legs are short relative to body length, and there is extensive webbing between the toes on the hind feet.** Females can grow to approximately 100 mm and males to approximately 75 mm SVL.

Variation: Ventral pigmentation is most intense on older/larger frogs and often is

weak or absent on juveniles. Albino and unspotted individuals are known.

Eggs and Larvae: The globular-shaped egg masses are approximately 60–100 mm in diameter, contain 200–800 embryos and usually are deposited communally. Each egg, inclusive of the surrounding membranes, is greater than 8 mm in diameter. Tadpoles have eyes inset from the margin of the head. Hatchlings are a uniform dark brown with external gills and are approximately 7–9 mm TL. Older tadpoles are dark brown to black dorsally and silver or white ventrally; magnification reveals brassy/gold flecking over much of the body surface. The tail fin extends onto the posterior one-third of the body. Tadpoles may reach 45–80 mm TL at high-elevation sites but 100 mm TL at some low-elevation sites.

Similar Species: Northern Red-legged Frogs have eyes oriented to the side and are prominently mottled in the groin region. Cascades Frogs are yellow on the undersides of the legs and abdomen, and their eyes are oriented to the sides. Northern Leopard Frogs have light "halos" around the dark spots. Pacific Treefrogs possess toe pads, and Boreal Chorus Frogs have a dark lateral stripe extending from the tip of the snout to the groin on both sides. Bullfrogs lack both dorsolateral folds and reddish coloration on the undersides.

Distribution: Columbia Spotted Frogs range from southeastern Alaska to central Nevada, and east to Saskatchewan, Montana, western Wyoming and north-central Utah. In Washington, Columbia Spotted Frogs occur at elevations ranging between 520 m (near Rock Lake, Whitman County) to 950 m (at Hart's Pass, Whatcom County). In Oregon, they range from 660 m (in the Powder River drainage near Richland, Baker County) to 2210 m (at Lost Lake, Elkhorn Ridge, Baker County), and in Montana to 2895 m (at Finger Lake, Park County).

Adult
*Chelan County,
Washington*

WILLIAM LEONARD

Adult
*Ravalli County,
Montana*

WILLIAM LEONARD

Adult
*Harney County,
Oregon*

WILLIAM LEONARD

Underside of an adult
*Okanogan County,
Washington*

**Communally deposited
egg masses**
*Kittitas County,
Washington*

Tadpole
*Okanogan County,
Washington*

Life History: Breeding occurs in late winter or spring shortly after ice-free water appears at breeding sites. Timing, however, varies regionally with climate. In the Columbia Basin, Washington, breeding typically occurs in March or April, but at high-elevation sites it may not occur until May or late June. Columbia Spotted Frogs often lay their eggs communally, and it is common to find 25 or more egg masses piled together. Eggs hatch after 12–21 days when the mean water temperature is 10–15.7°C. Hatchlings emerge and cling to the remains of the gelatinous egg masses. After a week or more, the small tadpoles begin swimming and feeding. The tadpoles metamorphose into froglets in their first summer or fall. Mortality of eggs, tadpoles and metamorphs can be as high as 95%. In Oregon, males reach sexual maturity at 21 months; females mature a year later. Oregon frogs regularly live 8 or 9 years. In Idaho, they are relatively long-lived, with adults regularly reaching 12 years of age.

Natural History: Individuals typically breed in the same sites in successive years. Males arrive first, congregating in breeding areas, vocalizing advertisement calls in a series of 3–12 rapid "tapping" notes. These calls may attract females and repel other males. Some females arrive at the breeding site already in amplexus with a male. Other females may enter a breeding area alone, where they are approached by and subsequently paired with males. The duration of amplexus may last from a few hours to days or even weeks. During egg-laying, the female releases her complement of eggs into the water while the male, still clinging to the female, releases sperm upon the ova. Egg masses are deposited atop matted grasses or are free-floating among herbaceous plants. Occasionally, eggs are deposited in slow-moving water in streams. Eggs may protrude above the water surface, resulting in mortality by freezing or desiccation. Following breeding, adults disperse into adjacent habitats. Adult frogs overwinter in ice-covered or partially frozen ponds, rivers and streams, and seeps. Frogs in ponds and rivers are active all winter, even under ice. Some frogs return to the breeding ponds in the fall, and the remainder return in the spring prior to breeding. Diet of adults includes aquatic and terrestrial invertebrates. Other frogs, including Pacific Treefrogs and young Columbia Spotted Frogs, also are eaten. In turn, Columbia Spotted Frogs may be preyed upon by various birds, mammals and gartersnakes. Tadpoles are consumed by dragonfly larvae, predaceous diving beetles, fish, gartersnakes, kingfishers and wading birds. Leeches have been seen consuming embryos. Adults sometimes emit "alarm calls," consisting of a prolonged (approximately 5–7 second) shriek, given when attacked; this may startle a predator and cause it to lose its grip.

Habitat: The Columbia Spotted Frog is usually found near water. The species breeds in relatively exposed, shallow waters (< 60 cm) of sedge fens, riverine overbank pools, beaver ponds and small lakes. Vegetation in the breeding pools generally is dominated by herbaceous plants.

Remarks: The destruction of wetland habitat for development and agriculture has long been the primary threat to Columbia Spotted Frogs. Livestock grazing and non-native fish may pose additional threats. In Idaho, the density of this species was significantly lower in high-elevation lakes with introduced trout than in fishless lakes. In Oregon, however, habitat quality exerted more influence on the abundance of eggs and larvae of this frog than the presence of trout in high-elevation lakes.

NORTHERN LEOPARD FROG

Rana pipiens   SCHREBER

Author: Kelly R. McAllister

Description: Adults and juveniles are easily recognized by their **large, oval-shaped spots, each surrounded by a light halo.** Northern Leopard Frogs' skin is smooth, and the **dorsolateral folds are light in color and prominent.** Undersides are creamy white, with no dark pigmentation. Adult males range from 50–80 mm SVL, females from 65–100 mm.

Variation: Northern Leopard Frogs can have a green or a brown background color, or a combination of green and brown. Spots may be reduced or absent in some young frogs.

Eggs and Larvae: Eggs are laid in an oblong mass, about 75–150 mm long by 50–75 mm wide, composed of 1000 to 7000 eggs. Each egg, including the surrounding membrane, is less than 8 mm in diameter. Tadpoles are dark brown or gray dorsally and creamy white on the central underbelly. Brassy flecks are scattered on the back, coalescing into coarse, metallic speckling on the sides. The tail fin is transparent, with scattered light flecking.

Similar Species: Because of the distinctive large dark spots with light borders and the bright, full, dorsolateral folds, this frog is unlikely to be confused with any other. However, tadpoles are difficult or impossible to distinguish reliably from those of other *Rana*. Because of range overlap, Northern Leopard Frog tadpoles are most likely to be confused with Columbia Spotted Frog tadpoles, which have finer, more silvery flecking on the sides, rather than the coarse, gold or brassy pigments that appear on the sides of Northern Leopard Frog tadpoles. To distinguish Northern Leopard Frog tadpoles from those of treefrogs and chorus frogs, look down from above. The eyes of the Northern Leopard Frog are slightly inside the margin of the outline of the head. Treefrog and chorus frog eyes protrude beyond the margin.

Distribution: The Northern Leopard Frog is widely distributed in North America, occurring across Canada from Saskatchewan east to Newfoundland, south to West Virginia, southwest to northern Arizona and California and northwest to Washington and British Columbia. However, western populations have been disappearing, and the species is becoming quite rare west of the Continental Divide. Only one population in British Columbia (near Creston), one in eastern Washington (Crab Creek), one in Oregon (Vale), one in California (Owens Valley) and two in western Montana are currently known. Populations occur at elevations from near sea level to 3350 m. In the western region covered

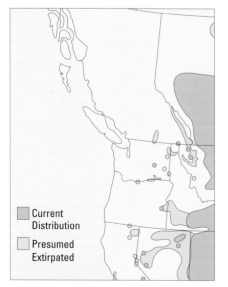

Current Distribution

Presumed Extirpated

Adult
*Glacier County,
Montana*

WILLIAM LEONARD

Adult
*Grant County,
Washington*

WILLIAM LEONARD

Portrait of an adult
*Glacier County,
Montana*

WILLIAM LEONARD

Singing male
Michigan

Egg mass
*Grant County,
Washington*

Tadpole
*Grant County,
Washington*

by this book, only southern Idaho has a significant number of populations.

Life History: Breeding occurs during April in most of the west. Eggs are laid in globular masses attached to grass or other vegetation in shallow water. Eggs hatch in 2–3 weeks, and the small, gilled hatchlings cling to vegetation, living off their yolk sac for several more days before beginning to swim about, graze on algae and occasionally scavenge. In 58–105 days, the tadpoles develop all four legs and complete their transformation into frogs. By the end of their first summer, they can be relatively large, often 40–50 mm SVL. Some males likely breed the following spring, while females require an additional year.

Natural History: During breeding, adults congregate in suitable breeding sites, often shallow ponds with aquatic vegetation. While floating in shallow water, males advertise their positions with a wide repertoire of grunts and chuckles. The warmest part of the pond, frequently > 20°C, is often favored by congregations of males. Females approach and are clasped from behind. Eggs and sperm are released simultaneously. After breeding, adults disperse from the breeding sites, spacing themselves along water margins or in the moist shade of dense, low vegetation. Adults make considerable use of uplands during the summer. Juveniles disperse up to 5 km from source ponds. Juveniles are more easily observed than adults, primarily because of greater abundance and, perhaps, a greater tendency to bask. In winter, Northern Leopard Frogs move to relatively deep (often 1–3 m) portions of lakes, large ponds or streams and spend the winter nestled in rocks or mud, often at temperatures just above freezing. A telemetry study in Washington found four adults buried under several inches of soil and debris during fall, suggesting the possibility of overwintering underground. During winter, the frogs

remain motionless though capable of moving away if disturbed. In one Michigan study, home range varied from 68–503 square meters. Diet consists of a great variety of invertebrates, mostly insects, though vertebrate prey such as small birds and gartersnakes have been found in stomachs. Northern Leopard Frogs are frequently mentioned as important prey for gartersnakes. Sympatric amphibian species include Pacific Treefrog, Long-toed and Tiger Salamanders, Columbia Spotted Frog and Great Basin Spadefoot.

Habitat: Shallow permanent or semi-permanent ponds (usually < 5 ha), slow-moving streams with shallow, marshy borders, or extensive marshes are needed for breeding. Gravel pits, stock ponds and beaver ponds are commonly used for breeding. Uplands with extensive grass or shrub cover are ideal habitat, although meadows interspersed with forest are also suitable, as long as breeding habitat is available nearby.

Remarks: Not only are leopard frogs found in much of North America, they have historically been shipped live over great distances to biological supply vendors and the many schools that use frogs in the classroom. As a result, individual frogs and populations of frogs may have their origins well outside our region. Leopard frogs inhabiting a small pond on the campus of Washington State University are locally known to have been established through releases of frogs left over from biology classes. In the west, Northern Leopard Frogs historically occupied aquatic environments within arid regions. Perhaps the patchy, fragmentary nature of their habitat in this region predisposed them to local extinction. In any case, the precise reasons for their widespread decline in the west are unknown. Drought, habitat loss, fertilizers, pesticides and predation or competition from introduced species are oft-proposed causes.

OREGON SPOTTED FROG

Rana pretiosa　　　BAIRD AND GIRARD

Authors: William P. Leonard and Kelly R. McAllister

Description: This robust frog is olive, brown or brick red, with **large, irregularly shaped spots on the back, sides and legs. The spots, which frequently have light centers, have indistinct edges.** Small bumps and tubercles sometimes cover the back, and a dorsolateral fold runs along each side of the back. **The chartreuse-colored eyes are decidedly upturned.** The **lower abdomen and undersides of the hind legs are colored with varying amounts of a red or orange pigment that appears painted on.** The groin is **not mottled.** The hind legs are relatively short, and **when a leg is adpressed forward, the heel does not extend beyond the nostrils.** There is extensive webbing between the toes on the hind feet. Sexually mature females range between 60 and 100 mm SVL, and males between 45 and 75 mm SVL. Recently metamorphosed Oregon Spotted Frogs range from 20–30 mm SVL.

Variation: Dorsal color varies among populations. Frogs tend to redden with age, with larger ones often having a brick red color. Juveniles typically have red or orange pigments limited to the undersides of the hind legs.

Eggs and Larvae: Each egg mass is globular, measures approximately 60–100 mm diameter, and contains 400–700 eggs. Eggs, inclusive of jelly layers, average 8 mm in diameter, and an early-stage embryo is 2–2.5 mm in diameter, dark brown above and cream colored below. Hatchlings are dark brown with long gills. Tadpoles have dorsal-oriented eyes, are marked with fine dark flecks in the dorsal fin and metallic surface pigments on the tail musculature, and are white on the belly. Tadpoles can reach 110 mm TL before metamorphosing in their first summer or fall.

Similar Species: The Northern Red-legged Frog has longer hind legs, gold- or brown-colored and outward-oriented eyes, and a mottled groin with a greenish wash. The Cascades Frog is colored yellow on the belly and has outward-oriented eyes. The Columbia Spotted Frog is very similar in appearance, but its range does not overlap with that of the Oregon Spotted Frog.

Distribution: The Oregon Spotted Frog once occurred from southwest British Columbia through western Washington and Oregon into northeastern California. Today, the species has a much-reduced range and is known from only three localities in British Columbia, four localities in Washington and fewer than 30 localities in Oregon. It has been extirpated in California. In Washington, it occurs at elevations from 40–620 m, but in Oregon it is found between 1025 and 1600 m.

Life History: Breeding occurs February through March at lower elevations but

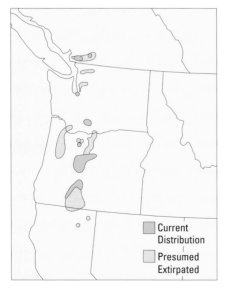

Current Distribution

Presumed Extirpated

Adult basking at overwintering site
Klickitat County, Washington

Adult
Deschutes County, Oregon

Adult at breeding site floating on egg masses
Thurston County, Washington

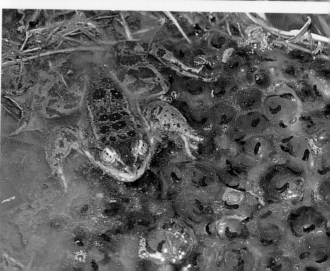

Underside of an adult
*Klickitat County,
Washington*

WILLIAM LEONARD

**Communally laid
egg masses**
*Thurston County,
Washington*

WILLIAM LEONARD

Tadpole
*Klickitat County,
Washington*

WILLIAM LEONARD

does not occur until March or April at higher elevations in the Cascade Range. Several weeks after the eggs are laid, thousands of hatchling tadpoles emerge and lie in the near liquefied jelly. Approximately one week after hatching, the larvae become free-swimming tadpoles, actively feeding upon algae, detritus and, in some cases, bacteria. Males begin to breed just prior to 2 years of age, while females breed at 3 years of age. Marking studies in lowland Washington indicate that annual survival of adults is less than 50%. At this rate, few frogs live beyond 5 years. Indeed, out of 180 frogs marked in 1997, only 3 were recaptured during the 2003 breeding season, when an intensive capture effort yielded more than 308 individuals. Two of these "old-timers" had been sub-adults in 1997. The third, a male, was a large adult in 1997, suggesting that he was a minimum of 8 years old in 2003.

Natural History: At breeding sites, males gather in "lek-like" groups, floating in the shallows and calling as they await the arrival of a female. Advertisement calls consist of a rapid series of 5–50 faint "tapping" notes. Most breeding takes place within a 2–3 week period. Females typically lay their egg mass adjacent to others, and some aggregations are composed of more than 100 egg masses. Egg masses are deposited in still, shallow water, unattached but resting on submerged herbaceous vegetation. Egg masses often protrude above the water's surface, which results in egg mortality if temperatures fall below freezing. After breeding, adults disperse into aquatic habitats in adjacent wetlands and riparian areas. Adults remain active year-round near sea level, though their winter activities are largely underwater. Cold temperatures apparently cause frogs to seek waters that remain aerobic, often with flow that prevents freezing. Adults feed upon arthropods (e.g., spiders, insects),

earthworms and other invertebrate prey. In turn, Oregon Spotted Frogs may be preyed upon by Mink, River Otter, Raccoon, herons, bitterns, corvids, gartersnakes and Bullfrogs, while tadpoles may be consumed by dragonfly larvae, predaceous diving beetles, fish, larval and paedomorphic salamanders, gartersnakes and wading birds. Rough-skinned Newts and caddis fly larvae occasionally eat eggs.

Habitat: Oregon Spotted Frog populations occur in association with relatively large wetland complexes. Breeding occurs in shallow, relatively unshaded, emergent wetlands. The breeding ponds, which are typically dry by mid- to late summer, range in depth from 5–36 cm during the breeding season and are vegetated by low-growing emergent species such as grasses, sedges and rushes. Summer habitats are more variable and include more heavily shaded sites with deeper water and abundant floating and submerged aquatic plants. Overwintering sites often have springs, particularly in areas where winter freezing is prolonged.

Remarks: Over the past half-century, this species has declined to the point that the species is now in jeopardy over most of its range. The most likely cause for this frog's precipitous decline is the hydrological modification and destruction (draining, flooding and filling) of large, shallow-water, emergent wetlands. Human achievements in suppressing fire, confining rivers and streams to stable channels, and eliminating Beaver have been harmful because natural disturbances create and maintain emergent wetland breeding habitats by setting back succession. Introduced predators, including sport fishes and Bullfrogs, also pose serious threats resulting from predation and competition for critical habitats.

WOOD FROG

Rana sylvatica   LeCONTE

Author: Elke Wind

Description: The Wood Frog reaches up to 60 mm SUL; females are slightly larger than males. **This species is recognized by its dark "mask," extending from the tip of the snout (through the eye) across the tympanum, bordered by a cream-colored upper lip line.** Dorsal coloration may be tan, reddish, brown, gray or almost black; females are often more reddish or lighter than males. Some animals are mottled, while others are uniformly colored. Most individuals have a light mid-dorsal stripe and 2–3 dark bars on the hind limbs. The ventral surface is usually mottled white, with a dark spot near the base of each forelimb. Wood Frogs have distinct dorsolateral folds running along the back, incomplete webbing between the toes of the hind limbs, and a tympanum that is one-half to approximately the same size as the eye. The skin is usually smooth, but tubercles may be present laterally. The limbs are relatively short in comparison to other ranids, especially in the north; the leg to heel measurement is equal to or shorter than the body length. Newly metamorphosed Wood Frogs average 16 mm in length and are similar in appearance to adults.

Variation: The species is highly variable in color, ranging from a tan to almost black dorsum. Some animals are mottled, while others are uniformly colored. The mid-dorsal stripe and dark bars on the hind limbs can be weak markings or absent.

Eggs and Larvae: Females lay an average of 800 eggs within a globular mass, approximately 5–7 cm in diameter, which becomes flat and spreading. Toward maturity, the egg mass becomes embedded with green algae. Eggs are attached to vegetation or laid freely, usually communally. Embryos average 1.6 mm in diameter, are dark above and cream colored below and are surrounded by a thin jelly layer so that they appear densely packed. Hatchlings are dark, with a narrow head, and long, visible gills. The gray or black tadpoles are deep-bodied, and the eyes are widely spaced on top of the head, near the body outline when viewed from above. There are dense, short rows of gold flecks near the mouth. The anus opens to the right (dextral), and the belly is dark. Tadpoles average 55 mm TL before metamorphosis. Tadpoles have a relatively short tail in relation to their body (≤ 1.5 times the body length). The dorsal fin begins posterior to the base of the tail trunk, which is dark along the upper edge and light below.

Similar Species: In northwestern North America, the Wood Frog may be confused with the Columbia Spotted Frog (*Rana luteiventris*). The spotted frog is larger (SUL to 100 mm), has light-centered spots and small bumps along the dorsum, and

Adult

Ingham County, Michigan

LARRY WEST

Adult

Ingham County, Michigan

JAMES HARDING

Adult

Ingham County, Michigan

LARRY WEST

Adult
*Ingham County,
Michigan*

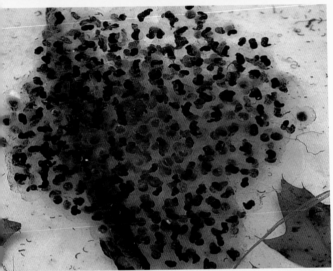

Egg mass
*Ingham County,
Michigan*

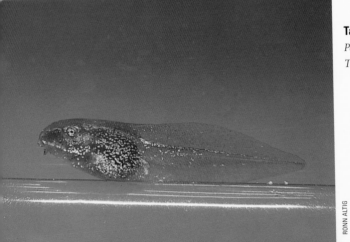

Tadpole
*Polk County,
Tennessee*

usually lacks the dark mask of the Wood Frog. The dorsolateral folds are incomplete on the spotted frog, the toes of the hind limbs have extensive webbing and the eyes are positioned higher on the head; they do not break the body outline when viewed from above. The egg mass of the Columbia Spotted Frog is slightly larger than that of the Wood Frog, and it is soft. The tail length of Columbia Spotted Frog hatchlings and tadpoles is longer, > 1.5 times the body length, and the belly is pale gold.

Distribution: The Wood Frog has an extensive range in North America, from Alaska east to the Atlantic coast and south to the Appalachians and Ozarks. It is the only North American amphibian found north of the Arctic Circle (to 69° N). Within the Northwest, it is common throughout much of interior British Columbia, the Yukon Territory and Alaska. The species is absent from coastal British Columbia, including the Queen Charlotte Islands.

Life History: Wood Frogs are explosive breeders in northern areas; reproduction occurs over 1–7 days in late April to early June. This species is often the earliest amphibian to breed, when ice has recently begun to recede and temperatures are just above freezing. This species has numerous adaptations for survival in cold environments, including rapid development in frigid waters. Hatching occurs approximately 3 weeks after egg deposition, when larvae are 7–10 mm in total length. Metamorphosis occurs 6.5–12 weeks after hatching. Wood Frogs reach sexual maturity at approximately 3 years of age in Alaska and 5 years (48 mm SUL) in the northeastern parts of their range. They may live for up to 10 years.

Natural History: Male Wood Frogs arrive at breeding sites first and emit a quack-like call that travels only a short distance. Calling may occur during the day or at night, but Wood Frogs are largely diurnal. Females tend to remain below the water surface during the breeding season. Male Wood Frogs can overwhelm females during the breeding season, inadvertently killing them in the process of mating. This species is freeze-tolerant due to the ability to flood its cells with glucose, a natural antifreeze. Adults feed on mollusks, earthworms, other invertebrates and occasionally their own young; flies and beetles appear to be a major component of the diet. These frogs are dependent upon camouflage to escape predation and are capable of remarkable color changes through shades of brown. Individuals emit a grating noise or "yeow" when handled. Wood Frog tadpoles and adults contain a toxin that makes them unpalatable to many predators.

Habitat: Wood Frogs are so named for their extensive use of terrestrial forested habitats. They appear to select ephemeral, fish-free ponds and marshes for breeding but also reproduce in lakes and the backwaters of streams. They lay their eggs at intermediate depths (e.g., 35 cm) in warmer edges of ponds. Within their extensive range, they occur in many habitats, including urban areas. They are predominantly forest-dwellers in the east but are more common in open areas in grasslands and tundra of the west. Hibernation is largely terrestrial, under leaf litter and humus, although some Wood Frogs overwinter underwater.

Remarks: The majority of the information we have on Wood Frogs comes from studies conducted in Alaska and eastern North America; no studies have been conducted on Wood Frog populations in British Columbia.

AMPHIBIAN ANATOMY

Figure 1. **Characteristics of Salamanders**

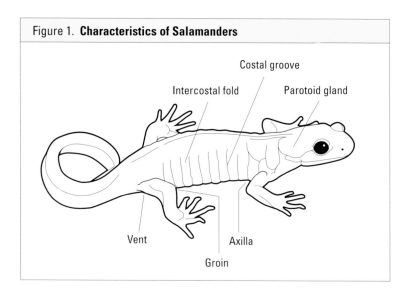

Figure 2. **Characteristics of Plethodontid Salamanders**

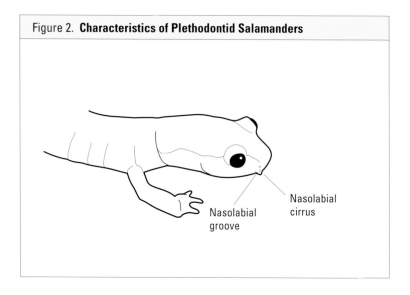

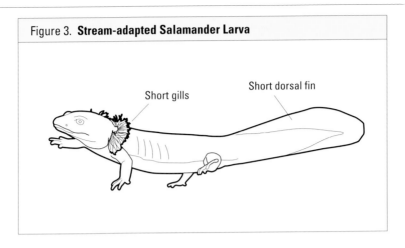

Figure 3. **Stream-adapted Salamander Larva**

Short gills

Short dorsal fin

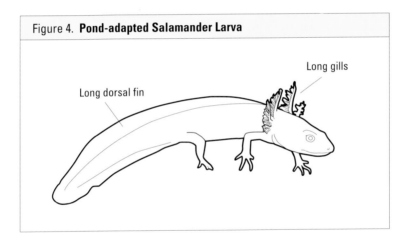

Figure 4. **Pond-adapted Salamander Larva**

Long gills

Long dorsal fin

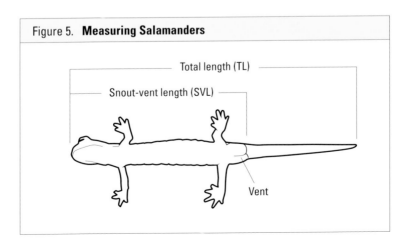

Figure 5. **Measuring Salamanders**

Total length (TL)

Snout-vent length (SVL)

Vent

Figure 6. **Identifying Characteristics of Frogs**

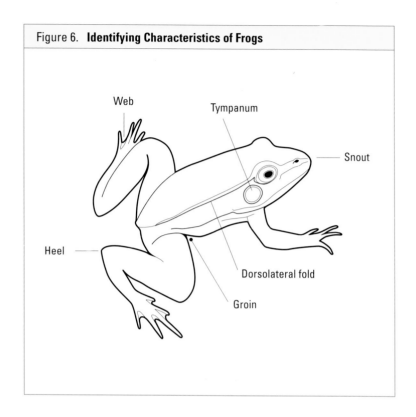

Figure 7. **Characteristics of Tadpoles**

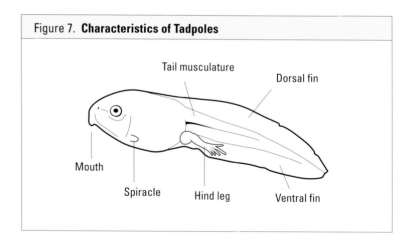

Figure 8. **Identifying Characteristics of Toads**

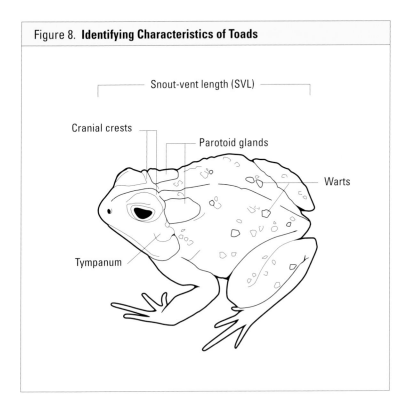

GLOSSARY

abdomen: Belly portion of an organism, posterior to the chest. Abdomen can also refer to the general area between the forelimbs and hind limbs.

adpressed limbs: When forelimbs are pressed backward and hind limbs are pressed forward, against the side of the body. Adpressing limbs is done to measure costal grooves or intercostal folds between the toe tips of fore and hind feet.

amplexus: Mating position of frogs, wherein the male clasps the back of a female with his forearms in position to fertilize the eggs of the female as she lays them.

anterior: Toward the front of the axis of the body (toward the head).

anuran: From the order Anura (which means "without tail"). As a noun, it means a frog or toad; as an adjective, it means relating to a frog or toad.

axilla: The lateral surface immediately posterior to the forelimb.

balancer: A structure found on the side of the rear of the head of some salamander larvae during their early life stages to help maintain balance in the water column. Balancers are found in lentic species.

biogeographic element: Assemblage of species associated with a specific geographic region.

caudate: From the order Caudata (which means "having tail"). As a noun, it means salamander or newt.

cloaca (plural: cloacae): The common urogenital (sexual function plus nitrogenous waste removal) opening of amphibians. It is also known as the **vent.**

colluvial: Pertaining to the streamside. For example, colluvial rock is that rock that originates from a bank or gorge.

conspecific: Member of the same species.

costal groove: The vertical slit on the lateral surface of salamanders that is used for passive water uptake. This indentation occurs between intercostal folds.

crypsis (adjective: cryptic): The phenomenon of blending in with surroundings.

demarcation line: In bi-colored animals, the point at which there is a separation of dorsal and ventral colors and/or patterns on the lateral surface.

disjunct: Separate or spatially removed. Disjunct distribution refers to populations that are isolated from one another and do not have genetic interchange.

diurnal: Active during the daylight hours.

dorsal (noun: dorsum): Pertaining to the upper surface ("back").

dorsolateral: The surface between the dorsal and lateral surfaces.

dorsolateral fold: Fold of skin along the dorsolateral surface of some frogs.

dorsoventrally flattened: Flattened dorsally to ventrally; basically somewhat flat in appearance.

ecotone: The transitional zone between two habitat types.

ectotherm: An organism that regulates its body temperature largely by exchanging heat with its surroundings.

embryo: An egg after fertilization. This is the earliest stage of development. Embryos become larvae.

endemic: Native species found only in a particular area.

estivate (also aestivate): To spend the summer in a torpid or dormant state.

explosive breeding: Mating behavior of certain amphibians, wherein adults arrive and occupy breeding sites in a short span of time. Explosive breeding may last only a few days.

fecundity: The capacity for procreation vigor. Low fecundity organisms typically have few eggs (or offspring) and/or large gaps in mating events.

fossorial: Living or spending extended periods underground.

froglet: Juvenile frog, recently metamorphosed.

gravid: Possessing eggs.

groin: The lateral surface of the body just in front of the hind limb.

herpetology: Study of amphibians and reptiles. **Herpetofauna** refers to reptiles and amphibians and is often abbreviated "herptiles" or simply "herps."

hybrid (verb: hybridize): A genetic cross between species.

intercostal fold: The folds of tissue between costal grooves of salamanders.

intergrade: A transition zone, an area where populations interbreed.

invertebrate: An animal without a backbone.

keratin: A tough protein substance that makes up hardened epidermal tissues.

larva (plural: larvae): The early form of an amphibian prior to transforming into the adult form. A tadpole is the larva of a frog.

lateral: Aligned along the horizontal axis of the body. Normally, this refers to the animal's side.

late-seral forest (also late-successional forest): A forest age class or successional stage with older, larger trees in the overstory (e.g., 100- to 500-year-old trees) and structural conditions including multiple canopy layers and dead wood that is both standing and "down."

lek: Breeding area where males congregate to attract female mates. Other resources such as food, shelter and nesting areas are generally not present at a lek.

lentic: Pertaining to standing water. Lentic habitat may also be called stillwater or wetland habitat, and includes ponds and lakes.

lotic: Pertaining to flowing water. Lotic habitat includes streams and seeps.

macroinvertebrate: Referring to "large" invertebrates (animals without backbones). In our context, this usually means aquatic insect larvae and other invertebrates that we can see well with the naked eye.

maxillary: Pertaining to the upper jaw.

melanistic: A pattern completely (or nearly) black or brown because of the presence of melanophores in the skin. **Amelanistic** is without black or brown pigments.

melanophore: Brown or black pigments found in the upper two surfaces of the skin.

mental gland: Pheromone gland on the chin of some male salamanders, used during courtship to deliver olfactory signals to a female to induce receptivity to breeding.

mesic: A moist habitat.

metamorph: A recently metamorphosed amphibian, or one in late-stage metamorphosis.

metamorphosis (verb: metamorphose): The process of undergoing significant morphological change, such as a tadpole (anuran larva) transforming into a frog. Salamanders undergo a less dramatic metamorphosis

mitochondrial DNA: Genetic material found in the mitochondria of an organism's cells, rather than in the cell nucleus. Mitochondria are cellular organelles, thought to have been derived from primitive symbiotic bacteria, hence having their own DNA separate from the nucleus. Mitochondria replicate independently from the nucleus. They are inherited only from an organism's mother; thus the mitochondrial DNA represent only the matrilineal line. Examination of both nuclear and mitochondrial DNA helps to understand the phylogenetics of organisms.

modal (number): The value occurring most frequently, such as in the number of costal grooves most often seen in a population of salamanders.

morphology: The form and structure of organisms.

nasolabial cirrus (plural: cirri): An extension of fleshy tissues of the nasolabial groove area that is used for perception of chemical cues by male plethodontid salamanders.

nasolabial groove: A slit from the nostril to the mouth in plethodontid salamanders that is used for the uptake of chemical cues (pheromones) during mating activities.

nocturnal: Active during the night.

nuptial pad (also called tubercle): A thickened portion of skin on the forefeet or "thumbs" of some male anurans, used for grasping the female during amplexus.

overwinter: For amphibians, the period of time between fall and spring activity periods. This is a time of slowed activity that roughly corresponds to hibernation in mammals.

oviposition (verb: oviposit): Egg-laying.

paedomorphic (noun: paedomorph): Retaining larval characteristics (such as the retention of gills in certain salamanders) into adult life. This is also (basically) known as neoteny. Facultative paedomorphism is when the paedomorphic form occurs only under certain environmental conditions.

parotoid gland: Large dorsolateral glands of toads and some salamanders, which may exude toxins.

pathogen: A disease-causing organism, such as a bacterium or fungus.

pedicel: A tough gelatinous strand found on the upper surface of eggs in some salamanders. The pedicel is used to attach eggs to the ceiling of the nest chamber.

phylogenetic: Relating to the evolutionary development and taxonomic relationships of species.

plethodontid: Belonging to the family Plethodontidae, the lungless salamander family.

posterior: Toward the end of the axis of the body (toward the tail on a salamander).

premaxillary teeth: Teeth that are found in the anterior of the upper jaw (**premaxilla**). In some salamander species, these teeth overhang the lower jaw.

proximal: Nearer to the point of attachment or center part of the body.

refugium (plural: refugia): An area where a viable population exists; habitat providing cover or respite from adverse environmental conditions.

riparian: Habitat and vegetation surrounding aquatic systems, such as lakes, streams and rivers.

riverine: Pertaining to the environment of rivers (large lotic habitats).

***Saprolegnia* fungus:** Genus of a filamentous white fungus that infects aquatic organisms.

species: Organisms that are so closely related to one another that peer experts have agreed that these taxa should belong to the same basic category. Generally (not without exception), members of a species interbreed while they do not successfully breed with members of other species. Taxonomically, the species is the basic group wherein one form of organism is recognized as being distinct from another. The species concept has been challenged by scientists because of the artificial nature of categorization, as variation seems to be somewhat continuous, but the concept persists as the integral base for taxonomy, including in this book.

spermatophore: Sperm packet produced by male salamanders.

spiracle: The external gill opening of tadpoles.

subspecies: A group within a species that is distinct, usually corresponding to regional variation. A taxon lower in rank to the species.

SUL: Abbreviation for Snout-Urostyle Length, the length of an anuran from the tip of the snout to the vent or urostyle (posterior part of pelvis).

SVL: Abbreviation for Snout-Vent Length, a standard measurement of amphibians.

sympatric: Occurring in the same geographic range, often in the same local areas and basic habitats.

tadpole: A larval frog or toad.

taxon (plural: taxa): A taxonomic group of animals. For example, subspecies, species, families and orders are all different taxa.

taxonomy: The study of the relationship of organisms to one another through time.

TL: Abbreviation for Total Length. Standard measurement from the tip of the snout to the tip of the tail (salamanders) or posterior-most part of the body (anurans).

toadlet: Juvenile toad, recently metamorphosed.

traditional breeding sites: Where amphibians typically breed on a regular basis.

transform: Metamorphosis or transition between life stages. Some amphibians transform from aquatic larvae to terrestrial juveniles.

tubercle: A small, rounded bump.

tympanum: External eardrum of frogs.

vagility: The movement or dispersal ability of taxa. Low vagility taxa do not move very much.

vent: Same as **cloaca.**

ventral: Pertaining to the underside; also, **venter.**

vocal sac: An inflatable pouch below or on the sides of the throat of many male frogs which may act as a resonating chamber to amplify the calls.

vomerine teeth: Teeth on the vomer bone in the upper part of the mouth.

woodland salamander: A salamander of the genus *Plethodon.* Woodland salamanders are terrestrial salamanders commonly found in the Pacific Northwest and eastern United States.

GENERAL REFERENCES

Reading Material

Altig, R., R.W. McDiarmid, K.A. Nichols, and P.C. Ustach. *Tadpoles of the United States and Canada: A Tutorial and Key.* www.pwrc.usgs.gov/tadpole/

Bishop, S.C. 1947, 1995. *Handbook of Salamanders.* Ithaca, New York: Comstock.

Conant, R., and J.T. Collins. 1991. *Reptiles and Amphibians of Eastern/Central North America. Peterson Field Guides.* Boston: Houghton Mifflin Company.

Corkran, C.C., and C. Thoms. 1996. *Amphibians of Oregon, Washington, and British Columbia: A Field Identification Manual.* Redmond, WA: Lone Pine Publishing.

Crother, B.I. (chair). 2001. Scientific and Standard English names of amphibians and reptiles of North America north of Mexico, with comments regarding confidence in our understanding. Committee on Scientific and Standard English Names, Society for the Study of Amphibians and Reptiles. *Society for the Study of Amphibians and Reptiles Herpetological Circular* 29. http://www.ku.edu/~ssar/pdf/crother.pdf

Crother, B.I., J. Boundy, J.A. Campbell, K. De Quieroz, D. Frost, D.M. Green, R. Highton, J.B. Iverson, R.W. McDiarmid, P.A. Meylan, T.W. Reeder, M.E. Seidel, J.W. Sites, Jr., S.G. Tilley, and D.B. Wake. 2003. Scientific and standard English names of amphibians and reptiles of North America north of Mexico: update. *Herpetological Review* 34(3): 196–203.

Duellman, W.E., and L. Treub. 1986, 1994. *Biology of Amphibians.* New York: McGraw-Hill.

Dvornich, K.M., K.R. McAllister, and K.B. Aubry. 1997. Amphibians and reptiles of Washington State: location data and predicted distributions. Volume 2 in *Washington State Gap Analysis–Final Report*, eds. K.M. Cassidy, C.E. Grue, M.R. Smith, and K.M Dvornich. Seattle: Washington Cooperative Fish and Wildlife Research Unit, University of Washington.

Green, D.M., and R.W. Campbell. 1984. *The Amphibians of British Columbia. Handbook 45.* Victoria, British Columbia: British Columbia Provincial Museum.

Halliday, T., and K. Adler. 2002. *Firefly Encyclopedia of Reptiles and Amphibians.* Toronto, Ontario: Firefly Books.

Lannoo, M. (editor). 2005. *Amphibian Declines: The Conservation Status of United States Species.* Berkeley, California: University of California Press.

Maxell, B.A., J.K. Werner, P. Hendricks, and D.L. Flath. 2003. Herpetology in Montana: a history, status summary, checklist, dichotomous keys, accounts for native, potentially native, and exotic species, and indexed bibliography. *Northwest Fauna* 5. Olympia, WA: Society for Northwestern Vertebrate Biology.

McAllister, K.R. 1995. Distribution of amphibians and reptiles in Washington State. *Northwest Fauna* 3:81–112.

McDiarmid, R.W., and R. Altig (editors). 1999. *Tadpoles: The Biology of Anuran Larvae.* Chicago, Illinois: The University of Chicago Press.

Mead, L.S., D.R. Clayton, R.S. Nauman, D.H. Olson, and M.E. Pfrender. 2005. Newly discovered populations of salamanders from Siskiyou County, California, represent a species distinct from *Plethodon stormi. Herpetologica* 61:158–177.

Nussbaum, R.A., E.D. Brodie, Jr., and R.M. Storm. 1983. *Amphibians and Reptiles of the Pacific Northwest.* Moscow, Idaho: University of Idaho Press.

Olson, D.H., W.P. Leonard, and R.B. Bury (editors). 1997. Sampling amphibians in lentic habitats: methods and approaches for the Pacific Northwest. *Northwest Fauna* 4. Olympia, WA: Society for Northwestern Vertebrate Biology.

Petranka, J.W. 1998. *Salamanders of the United States and Canada.* Washington, D.C.: Smithsonian Institution Press.

Pough, F.H., R.M. Andrews, J.E. Cadle, M.L. Crump, A.H. Savitzky, and K.D. Wells. 2004. *Herpetology.* Upper Saddle River, New Jersey: Pearson-Prentice Hall.

Russell, A.P., and A.M. Bauer. 2000. *The Amphibians and Reptiles of Alberta: A Field Guide and Primer of Boreal Herpetology.* Calgary, Alberta: University of Calgary Press.

Shaffer H.B., G.M. Fellers, S.R. Voss, J.C. Oliver, and G.B. Pauly. 2004. Species boundaries, phylogeography and conservation genetics of the red-legged frog *(Rana aurora/draytonii)* complex. *Molecular Ecology* 13:2667–2677.

Stebbins, R.C. 2003. *A Field Guide to Western Reptiles and Amphibians.* Boston: Houghton Mifflin.

Stebbins, R.C., and N.W. Cohen. 1995. *A Natural History of Amphibians.* Princeton, New Jersey: Princeton University Press.

Twitty, V.C. 1966. *Of Scientists and Salamanders.* San Francisco: W.H. Freeman and Company.

West, L., and W.P. Leonard. 1997. *How to Photograph Reptiles and Amphibians.* Mechanicsburg, Pennsylvania: Stackpole Books.

Wright, A.H., and A.A. Wright. 1949, 1995. *Handbook of Frogs and Toads of the United States and Canada.* Ithaca, New York: Comstock Publishing Associates, Cornell University Press.

Zug, G.R., L.J. Vitt, and J.P.Caldwell. 2001. *Herpetology: An Introductory Biology of the Amphibians and Reptiles.* San Diego: Academic Press.

Web Resources

AmphibiaWeb.
http://elib.cs.berkeley.edu/aw/

Idaho Digital Atlas (amphibians)
http://imnh.isu.edu/digitalatlas/bio/amph/main/amphmnfr.htm

MacDonald, S.O. *Amphibians and Reptiles of Alaska: A Field Handbook.*
http://www.alaskaherps.info

Journals and Monographs

Copeia. Published quarterly by the American Society of Ichthyologists and Herpetologists. http://www.asih.org/

Herpetologica, and *Herpetological Monographs.* Published by the Herpetologists League. http://www.inhs.uiuc.edu/cbd/HL/HL.html

Journal of Herpetology, and *Herpetological Review.* Both published quarterly by the Society for the Study of Amphibians and Reptiles. http://www.ssarherps.org/

Northwestern Naturalist. Published quarterly by the Society for Northwestern Vertebrate Biology. http://www.snwvb.org

Northwest Fauna. Published occasionally by the Society for Northwestern Vertebrate Biology. http://www.snwvb.org

Northwest Science. Published quarterly by the Northwest Scientific Association. http://www.vetmed.wsu.edu/org_NWS/NWSci_Home.htm